DIRECTION ▲ NORTH

DIRECTION ▲ NORTH

A VIEW OF FINLAND

by

JOHN SYKES

CHILTON BOOKS

A Division of Chilton Company
Publishers
Philadelphia and New York

CONTENTS

ILLUSTRATIONS

"We are strong, but moderate. We are men of conscience."

"This light and silence is at the heart of Finland."

"To change, that's the problem. . . ."

"We are a winter people. . . . Winter makes strong."

"The Finns had the essence of champion runners."

"Good-bye to the past and to prayers offered beyond the grave."

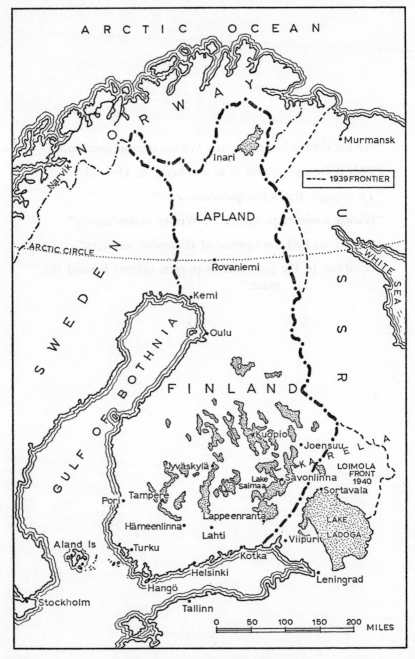

Finland and Her Neighbors

DIRECTION ▲ NORTH

1

AN ENCOUNTER DURING THE WINTER WAR

IT WAS still winter, and mostly night. Dusk filled the afternoons. Some days it snowed, on others the sun that splashed and sparkled through the forest till midday was swallowed in haze, and then before dark a dim red orb shone through. A clear sky brought out the planes, so the dull hours suited us best; we could sleep and eat and service the ambulances before the evening round began. That was our busy time.

One day the gong that sounded a minute before the planes came over had not sounded all afternoon. We had been playing cards and drinking coffee, and sharing our English cigarettes, and now we were sent to work on the cars. For a climate that was touching minus forty centigrade, and regularly hung around minus twenty, we wore felt boots and sheepskin coats, with layers of khaki woolens beneath, and white fur hats, and around our arms Red Cross flashes were pinned, and over all, even over the flashes, we wore white smocks that if the gong sounded would enable us as we groveled in the snow to look no different from it. Dress was pleasantly casual near the front—also for the Russians, as we had seen on their wounded, who were the only Russian prisoners we had seen, though their characteristic mark was the smell of birch tar about their boots. More important than dress in these frozen forests, where a peculiarly sinister war was being fought, was knowledge of the right password.

Our ambulances were hidden between trees, with extra branches laid over. The danger was, in the morning sun, that some window glass might become defrosted and reflect dazzle into the skies; for then all the surrounding wood, and worse, our seemingly deserted farmhouse, already bombed and seemingly unusable but in fact snug as a daytime hideout, would be bombed again and this time seriously; and the Finns harped on the possibility to show we too were subject to the Lord, and had better not forget it. We were careful even on this misty afternoon to keep to the one ski track by the road, so as to minimize our presence. It was a quarter-mile run from the farm to the trees that served us as a garage, with open land on either side. In peacetime it would have been a homely clearing, with cattle and horses and a sowing of oats to supplement the forest work, but in war it was abandoned. Some traffic had started along the road, horse sleighs heaped with hay, swishing and slithering on the icy surface. They came through the white drifts of fog rising from the hollows like sheep cascading through a dream, and as swiftly vanished. Then there were some lorries.

One got fuddled swinging the cars. Gloves stuck to the starting handles. The engines coughed, spat, and were silent. It was as well to get them working sweetly, for a halt on the road, with a traffic block and angry headlights and sentries screaming, had twice in our experience attracted Russian gunfire, a sudden shattering explosion of shells. We were learning all the points that could fail. Clutches and brakes and gears could go, but usually it was the petrol system, fed on petrol full of grit, that suddenly refused to function. I was at it now, unscrewing the feed and blowing through like a madman with an air pump, performing each move with doubled intensity to keep the stinging cold at bay. The frozen moisture in my nose tickled. I wrung my hands to revive circulation. I had removed my gloves, in some desperate maneuver, and so left skin sticking to the filter. But a gurgle of petrol suggested success. A last swing, and the ambulance started.

Word came for three of us to start early along the road. We returned first to the billet for our meal, safely cooked in this cloudy weather, and as it was Thursday the communal stockpot steamed with pea soup and pork, our weekly change from potato stew and beans, and maybe it was horsemeat but never enough that we could be sure about that. The pork tasted good on Thursdays. Thursday was also a milk-drinking day; so after the pork and the milk and the soup, and the rye bread brought in from the snow that was a convenient unfailing larder, and plenty of butter, and sugared coffee, and some of the jam that we had brought from England, and cheese and Quaker chocolate, and antiscurvy pills, we were especially ready, Thursday fit, for the work that would take us through the night to some hour of the following morning.

Night was our kingdom. The Russians ruled the day, except when the Finns outmaneuvered them, as at Suomassalmi and Tolvajärvi and, currently it was rumored, at a point to the south close by Lake Ladoga; but still the Russians ruled the skies, and on this stretch of the Loimola front, from the ant-high view of an ambulance driver, whose big Red Cross had been painted out with the wry comment that it drew attention, it was preferable to be abroad at night. Then too the planes came over, but the game was equal, the Finns saw to that.

They were schooled in every nuance of caution, and the road drill was strict.

We drivers each had a Finnish companion. Mine inevitably was known as Canada, as he had a brother who was mining there, who wrote letters in Finnish but among which the words *Kanada* and *kanadalainen* were translatable. Canada liked to say these words, in the inexpressive Finnish way, his pinched dour leathery features set, like the weather, below zero. When the winter wind blew at night, frosting the windscreen with whirls of hail, he said them, it could be, as consolation, as he clambered out of the heated cab to scrape the glass and take bearings on the road. He crooned them through the flat uneventful hours. Then as a sudden gift of surprise he would say *Kanada*, meaning that we were friends, or that indeed paradise existed and was a promise given to the faithful—as others might have used "Madonna" for all eventualities.

He knew the way, whatever the night, familiar it seemed with every tree, and he gave the password to the succession of sentries. He watched my driving without comment, except, as we hit ice or were adrift in snow or entered the deep ruts of the lorries, to make demonic steering movements, that were wilder and faster than those I was making, that were calculated to nerve me through but which afterwards he had difficulty in stopping. He blazed momentarily in this pantomime; but then he was back as dour as ever. All the Finns were Nuvularis, and some with much superior scorn. But Canada was a God-fearing man, and in most things this kept him modest.

Our meal concluded, we took to the road. We served a string of JSPs, or Regimental Aid Posts, at points behind the front somewhere in that area. I never got it more exact than that. Canada and I were the last to leave, the other cars disappearing in the mist. Once or twice the next ahead reappeared, as the lie of land favored visibility, and then it could be seen that our fellow ambulance was giving an extraordinary display, proceeding crabwise and seemingly bent on the deep soft bed of the ditch, only to swerve and rock and nearly topple and to proceed crabwise to the other edge. Then a moment later it was zigzagging with a bottom wobble like a terrified puppy, as once again it was swallowed up. Had it hit a tree? Was it lying on its side? Would it sheepishly return in the wrong direction? But there it was again, still performing its dance, coming and going through hallucinatory waves of softly blowing and clinging snow; and because of our amusement—well, mine, largely—it was some time before I realized that we were performing a similar dance. One took one's own course for granted.

The sky was clearing. There was a view of forest, and the snow whirling away at an angle; then it came down again, and now the traffic was thickening, and it took five minutes to nose past a bus crammed with stern, sour soldiers; and though there was no present danger from lights, there came the usual shout from an officer, and a slithering of sledges pulling to the side, and the sudden rearing and blowing of horses; then some minutes later it took only seconds to shoot past a lorry. These lorries, usually with full lights blazing, made three double journeys a night; they had to go through. They aimed along the lip of the ditch, or glanced at speed against ploughed-up snow (as you had to do), and for headlong seconds you were each burrowing into your wall that might behind the snow be rock, and there was always a terrible crunching and screech, but it was so quick you were past and again shaking on to the road proper; or they thundered up behind, and nudged and scraped till as quickly their lights were sweeping ahead, illuminating the whitened trees and at ground level the debris of war, the riddled cars and crippled tanks and barbed wire and mounds of dead. All along the way there were dead, visible in frozen stacks. There was no other solution for the moment.

It was certainly the harshest of winters. We were young enough to think it fun. But we were not, for all our service on the spot, implicated as were the Finns. Over five centuries they had fought the Russians. We had heard them say: "Once again we must do it . . . it is the contest to which God has called us . . . such adversity suits our nature."

They had no fear, these northern Ironsides.

The JSP was a group of tents down a track overhung with firs. In the principal tent the doctor waited, a Captain, together with his orderlies. The wounded that arrived on sleighs had mostly arm or leg wounds or an occasional scalp laceration, for the enemy were not offered large targets; or if a direct hit were scored, the victim died of shock in that cold. The patients sat on brushwood along one side of the tent, their bandaged limbs or heads adding to the rigidity of their posture. They were awaiting transfer to the ambulance, but they sat as though carved for eternity. The orderlies cleaned equipment and talked to Canada in undertones and tended the stove that formed the centerpiece of the tent, small logs being fed into its casing that ran up from a ground spike to the chimney and spark catcher at the crown. The smells were rank, but the warmth was good, and unless there was suddenly an urgent case we waited there till a later hour.

The doctor was friendly and spoke perfect English. He was immaculate, almost precious in grooming, with a tall golden face and beard, and though he was brisk and remote while tending with great expertise each wounded man, afterwards he liked conversation. I was surprised that he should treat with equality a mere ambulance driver, and I knew that Canada did not approve and would be more than usually glum afterwards; but then, of course, I was a foreigner, and English, and a volunteer, and like himself I came of a textile-manufacturing family, and the doctor, with his urbanity of speech gathering these and many other facts into a glow of sympathy between us, insisted on this evening talk. He kept my glass of tea filled. He was attentive and forever with light apology changing the angle of approach to a topic, building it up with contrasting touches. He was skeptical, he made a great point of being fair-minded, and he was perhaps more self-questioning than he knew. He was a Swedish Finn—I call him Lars Stromfors—and towards the Swedes, and his own caste in Finland, and in particular towards his own family, he was more than inclined to be deprecating. He was always saying, "My fam-

ily would be furious if they were to hear me say this . . .
they are not sufficiently fair-minded"; then again, "Where
are the Swedes? How many times in five hundred years
have we Finns fought their battles for them? They prefer,
exactly as Prussia over Poland, to settle with the Kremlin
at our expense." A minute later he was toning down this
judgment. He was passionately patriotic and he scoffed
as "Swedish business morality"—indeed, this further reflected on his conception of himself as a Swedish Finn
within Finland—but he never left a strong opinion unchanged. He chipped and modified until it was harmless.
It had something, especially when conversing with an
Englishman, to do with his sense of good form.

"You are early," he welcomed me that evening. "It is
good. We can talk. Please excuse me for some minutes."
He called an orderly to pour me tea. Canada across the
tent was scowling. Yes, for Canada, Stromfors was firstly
the name of one of the big bourgeois families—one of the
butchers, as the workers had called them, in the Civil
War of two decades earlier—so, with memories dying hard
in this climate, it was not easy for him to accept a mate
hobnobbing with one of their kidney. The rift in society
still ran deep. We had heard something of this at the
billet, from our interpreter, who made black jokes about
the state of Finnish life. And with the doctor himself
it was a constant topic, albeit with him it was laced with
apologies, circumlocutions, the ideal of frankness. It was
just possibly his basic topic, and bound up with revolt
from his family.

He joined me at his table. "I must tell you I enjoy
these evening conversations together. Is your tea still hot?"

His usual phrases which, in these circumstances of war and winter, never seemed repetitious. His smile shone with student gregariousness, with a wistful Nordic *angst* and willingness to dip into the soul's recesses. "I have heard from my uncle in Stockholm," he said; "he is there on business. Naturally! Though I suppose he has to go. War contracts. It seems the whole thing's finished, however. The Germans are determined that we come to terms with Russia. We shall not get supplies from England. America is too far away. Strange, all these people in the tent think that we are defeating our Neighbor. We have killed so many Ivans and Ivanovs. But then, there are so many more. Inescapably, we have to live with that."

"What will happen?"

"They will dictate the peace. Our frontiers will recede again—I would guess, to the limits of 1721. But mulishly we shall keep our autonomy; we have not been 'solved' like Latvia and Estonia. On the contrary, we have taught Molotov a lesson."

"Do you hate the Russians?"

"How can I hate them? They are men like myself; I dress their wounds. I see how poor and uncouth they are. Winners or losers, they will still be subject to a terrible enslavement of the mind. Though, if they encourage our Finnish Communists, it will be less easy to be fair to them."

"You fear they might back an internal revolt?"

"Now? Well, there is always a danger. But war has brought a new understanding, and unity, to the Finnish people. We use the word *yksimielisyys:* that is, unity, or unanimity. We are *aseveljiä*, or battle comrades. Good words, for on them depends our hope of staying independent. For if again we were mortally divided, as we were, I think you know, in our Civil War, when Finn shot and executed Finn—and many of our present soldiers were in it, on opposing sides then—we could not stand up to Russia. Would we deserve to?"

"Do you remember the Civil War?"

"I?" He laughed. "Do I look so old?" His handsome, slightly vain features reddened. "I was only six at the time. I mean, do I look so old?"

I hastened to reassure him.

"Well, this war is aging us. But my family, of course, were White supporters. My father was a personal friend of Mannerheim. I was brought up on their point of view. It is both true and false, like the Red point of view. One has to be fair. . . .

"Though you know," he carried on, above my murmur of sympathy, "even six months ago it was not absolutely certain that the Left-wing forces in this country—I mean, the Social Democrats, the great party of the Left, and the Trade Unions, let alone the Communists—would rally to the bourgeois government to fight against our Socialist neighbor. So deep has been the rift. For, right through the thirties the excesses continued—fascist, I regret to say, too many of them. Yet now you see a country united. That is the miracle of this war."

"The main plank for the future?"

"Yes, precisely. For that we have not fought in vain. You know, we are touching the most interesting topic of how Finns will go on from here, once peace is finally secure. I think it will depend on the men of the Left—not the Communists, but the Social Democrats; can they, and quickly enough, become statesmen, at each level of the country's life? That is the big question. And the dangers won't lessen."

And as if to underlie this proviso there was a rattle of machine-gun fire outside, and a lonely shell came whistling over, to die muffled somewhere in the forest. The Neighbor, the threat, was a constant factor.

"Now I would like to give you an instance," said the doctor, "of the sort of man I have in mind. A mechanic, but potentially a Minister. A man from Tampere, like myself—just a working man, but a terrific fighter. My father and uncles consider him an enemy. He was only finally allowed at the front so as to get shot—no, that is unfair! But in any case, here he has astonished with his readiness to go out and scalp the Russians; he hadn't been seen as that sort of fighter. He has been decorated. He could be an officer—except that he would never be an officer. He hates our guts. He sticks to his principles. I see him as a man of the deepest morality. I admire him. He is a contemporary hero."

"A war hero?"

"Oh more than that. In ten, twenty years from now he is the sort who must speak for Finland!"

He paused, his glow extending for an instant, then it was curbed; he smiled apologetically. "Perhaps . . . in these subarctic evenings, so remote . . . you think I exaggerate? No! What I am telling you is true. It is not for the sake of opposing my family." His apology became embarrassing. "Through this war I see objectively. Indeed, I myself remain a bourgeois." He colored again. "Let us drink more tea." He obviously felt that he had exceeded good form.

We were saved from trying to find, after this, the right note for continuing discussion by the entry of a senior doctor, a Major, who supervised this area medically and from time to time looked in. I promptly got to my feet and began fading into the background. But "Good evening," he greeted me, in a harsher English, and with an eye that checked over my dress, sardonic as it lighted on the Red Cross and the FAU of Friends Ambulance Unit. He had asked me before for a statement of our views, with the same air as the judge at the tribunal: how could we conscientiously object to standing up to a brutish invader? "And if you meet a caterpillar man, a Russian parachutist, who points his gun? Well? After you, he will shoot the wounded who are helpless in your ambulance. So? For their sake, you will carry a revolver. No? I find it outside my understanding." Since that time, whenever we had met (and I heard the same from my fellow drivers) he briskly avoided more than a nod that, grudgingly perhaps, did concede that, guns or no, we were carrying on and fulfilling our assignment.

This evening however he indicated that I should stay put for some further questions. He inspected the tent with Captain Stromfors. He was a head shorter, and broader in the cheeks, with cool steely gray eyes, which when for some second he paused—for he could not be said ever to relax—turned impossibly melancholic. As it seemed to be with all the Finns (the Major was a Finnish Finn), he was totally in love with his somber country, that might be blue and silver in spring but which now, here, in its blanket of snow, with the haggard air of war over it, was something most outsiders would run from. But these Finns nursed it within their souls, the essential Finland we could not see.

He returned to the table. From his pocket he took a tin, and from that he selected a number of scalpels. He took similar scalpels from an antiseptic tray, and laid them all side by side. "Can you tell me, please, which are the Russian knives?" It became apparent that he was asking me.

I pointed at the obviously cruder scalpels.

"Just so. Those are the Russian knives." His face darkened with a sort of fury. "Have you heard the news? Do you hear news from England? Your English radio news is preparing us to make peace with Mr. Stalin. Like the Swedish news, like the German news! So, unless we prefer to die, our doctors will have to use knives like that! We are being pushed out into darkness."

"Major," urged Stromfors, "there could be no question——"

"So we prefer to die! To a man. Even you, sir, as you are here. Even though you do not defend yourself." He quietened abruptly. "I cannot believe it."

He sat down. Some minutes later, on a captured and scratchy Russian gramophone, he was listening to captured Karelian music. "They claim it as theirs. We know it to be ours. It is the same music. So why do we fight?" He turned from the subject with dignified sorrow. After that the tent was still.

While he was present, some wounded came. One man

had a bullet in the stomach. Another had lost a part of his ear, while another, who at first looked forlornest, had nothing worse than rheumatism. At the end, swathed in blankets and topcoats, and attended by a comrade as though here were one for whom no respect was too great, was a bulky figure with a broody face, flattened by shock, a bulldog face in which defiance was momentarily quiescent. The Captain deftly dealt with each casualty, with the Major watching him in silence. The latter's cheekbones jutted more prominently in an attitude of frozen fatality; and at that moment every man in the tent, as though their officers' scandalous rumor had seeped through the barrier of language to them, from an English they did not know to Finnish, so that once again they stood revealed as victims of their history—that not even that winter's superhuman efforts had sufficed to shift a little in their favor, and that now if a truce were imminent turned each continuing casualty into waste—every one of them, as though on a frieze, reflected the same catatonic gloom, in a hitherto unplumbed reach of muteness.

We were told now to load the ambulance. On one side the racks were collapsed to make a bench for the sitting cases, on the other the two stretchers rested, with the stomach-wounded patient coughing above, and below the stocky bulldog man, still, it could be, wrestling with the affront of his first major physical indignity. One knee had been smashed to pieces with multiple fractures further down, and his right hand had been partially severed. One could imagine his awareness moving dumbly up and down between the wounds, raging yet already determining their cure, and in the meantime casting about for all the remaining soundness he could muster on which to secure his personality. Beneath his stupor, passion flickered that not even the shot of morphine canceled. The doctor had fixed emergency dressings, and a cardboard splint with light bandaging, and on the stretcher, to cushion the leg, we had placed a soft padding of hay. Below him and above were a quantity of blankets, to keep him warm and to ease his breathing. We took our cue from all who were tending him and settled him in with an extra care.

Captain Stromfors followed us out, dressed up now in a high fur collar. "That's the one that I was telling you about. The mechanic. The Socialist from Tampere. Take good care of that man." His philosophic, urbane countenance took on more strength than I had seen there previously. He checked the disposition in the ambulance, then the track now visible ahead, then some way into the surrounding forest. The sky had been clearing up alarmingly. Stars could be seen. The mist had lifted. There was no chance of an easy journey.

"I will see you tomorrow. Keep a good lookout. Especially, if this war is over . . . we need every hand for the coming peace." Despite his tone, his look stayed grave. He nodded to me to be on my way. In the mirror I could see him staring after, even praying perhaps, though that would be agnostically, for the wounded man he set such store by.

We turned off the track into the road. The spate of

traffic was faster than ever, rustling and hurtling through nighttime Karelia. The eternity of forests gleamed in the starlight. We had not gone a hundred yards before the first sentries were shouting. *"Valet pois!"* Out with your lights! We lumbered on, watchful, waiting. Then came the drone of the planes, high or low it was difficult to conjecture, but in the kind of number that made you hear them.

Driving by starlight was a different exerience from driving in snowfall. Even without lights one could see the vicinity, ghostly lit with its battle junk. Macabre objects that in the mist loomed up with poetic horror, like a single stack of bodies, or a single tank, still with the timber that had crippled it thrust between its wheels, or a pillbox or the contortions of wire or a single grim white-clad figure that for marooned seconds one feared to be a Russian, now reproduced themselves in quantity. There were lines of such tanks, rusting, rotting, cemeteries of wire, of abandoned defenses, and multitudes of soldiers dead and alive quartered in the unending glades. The whole operation weighed more on one, its range along the frontiers, the place names involved, the rivers, the lakes, the destroyed villages, and to our rear the chain of blacked-out cities with their grieving but tireless population—all this was suddenly apparent, drawn into one's driving perspective.

Of course, even now, when one could see the road, could see the frantic convoys of sleighs and brace oneself for a flurry of lorries, it didn't much help to know this was Syskyjärvi, then Pyörittäjä, then Leppäsyrjä, then Suistamo, and so down the line; for still, as in a treasure hunt, what mattered was the turn following the bridge, the sharp fork right, the manor house, after which one had to count a kilometer, then turn left, then be ready for the sentry. But, this attended to, this working script, one was forced by the starlight to broaden one's horizon, to realize Finland pitted against Russia and, beyond, the whole of tortured Europe feeling its way into the abyss. It was the beginning of March 1940.

The sentries were unusually jumpy this evening. We had resumed the use of lights, but again they were shouting. One man, whose mustache was frozen, an icy twirl above his lips, nearly broke the windscreen with his rifle. We had to creep forward by the stars. *"Perkele!"* swore Canada, scores of times. His annoyance with me was swallowed up by anger at this lingering delay. There was a Lotta waiting to see him at the hospital, and nothing less than a lorry's speed would have assuaged his hunger, and that without thought of the wounded. Whenever we heard their groans he shrugged, or seemed to concentrate the more on his girl. *"Perkele! Perkele!"* Then he hissed through his teeth, *"Ollapa Kanadassa!"* Which meant something like, "Oh to be in Canada!" It was strange to think of this leathery fellow attracting to himself the gaze of a Lotta at a time when men and even officers were available ten to a penny. There must be beauty beneath his dourness.

We were reaching the open ground near our billet. From here we had a wide view to various points along the railway line running from Loimola to the base area. The nip of land between Ladoga and Janisjärvi was lit by cascades of flares, and to the north as with a giant chandelier, toward Soanlahti and even Värtsilä, the Russians had opened up the skies. Pyrotechnically it was almost daylight, and not a healthy situation. The bombs were raining down here and there. It seemed haphazard from the edge of the forest, and in fact little damage was done at night, but as I knew from previous runs along the road once you were committed to an open stretch or the passage of a bridge or a railway station those bombers appeared immediately to know of it and to direct their sense of fun at you. You were glad the road itself was so tricky; that steadied some of your attention.

We were passing the billet. The Vanrikki's car was planted in the bay beside it. Had he taken leave of his senses? The Vanrikki, or Second Lieutenant, ruled this daytime roost of ours, and his most imperative command, always arrogantly expressed, was that no mark of car or man had ever to be spotted near it. Always before daylight someone checked that ski tracks were not indicative, and scattered snow over telltale bootsteps; and during the day, when we had had our sleep and wanted to relieve nature in the bogs, an eight-seater across the yard so frozen up an axe was kept there, and a plane, to control the height of turd that rose in eight frozen pinnacles, it was an operation requiring permission—one by one allowed to go over—and then by the shadows till the last jump, that was always watched to see that it did not enlarge the single dark mark; and then, if then the gong sounded, the unlucky ones still over there had to stay and to freeze above the icy pinnacles until the all clear was given. I remember, it was in one such fell situation that one of our chaps, a practical joker, and a bit mad with the cold and the strain, ignited a strip of *Daily Express* and floated it down the channel of urine running beneath the other seven bottoms. So agonized were they all feeling that they had not noticed what he was up to. Then, too late, they stayed glued above the flames, lest these should lead to greater danger.

But what about the Vanrikki's car? Oh, probably one of his own men, from this corps of Finnish drivers and orderlies whom we were assisting and relieving, would be detailed to cover up the tracks. One could see him, stiffly, hypercritically, face fixed with pride and fatigue, rapping out the order. He would like to give it to one of us—he despised the British and respected the Germans —but his sergeant more tactfully would allot it to a Finn. Any of those men would feel honored to do it. They worshipped their Vanrikki with his disdainful ways, for he was an outstanding athlete, and a daredevil, and was carrying on to the full with a Lotta. In fairness, as Stromfors would say, one must add that his charm, when he wished, could be devastating.

He must have worked to an interior model based firstly on the Jäger tradition (of German-trained Finns in the First World War, one of whom had been his father) and then on that of Hapsburg Vienna. Heel-clicking, insult, and devilry with women belonged absolutely to him, as did more purely Prussian zeal in one hundred per cent operational standards. There we failed him, rarely passing ninety. So we felt the continual lash of his scorn.

We knew all about him from the Légionnaire, as we

called the cook, whom it is a delight to mention as he was an opposite type of Finn. Though he also was a reckless fellow, an ex-seaman, an explorer (he assured us), with some knowledge of French as well as English, who whenever the sky clouded over put on his skis and went off to fish, breaking the ice in the nearest river. He alone among that group disliked the Vanrikki, and came gossiping to us, preferring our fog-bound front parlor where, encamped on the floor, we chatted and read and raided our iron ration of chocolate, to the more sober cardless, bookless atmosphere of the back room full of Finns. The Légionnaire was a Viipuri man, a Karelian, a talker, and his touch on the mandolin, when the mood took him, was tremulous and sad, full of high quivering hesitations that lapped over into silence. It was he who woke us up in the morning with a mock sergeant major's bark, or imitation of a Stuka diving. Each day he had some new turn.

Past the billet was Leppäsyrjä station. According to how the planes bombed it on the bright mornings they began their dive, or were flattening out, above the billet —that is, our seemingly abandoned farm—and relatively, though hideous, this was safer for us, for at night from higher up they lobbed their missiles with an airy casualness in passing, so that these exploded within a wide radius. This they seemed to do with all the stations, bridges, junctions, on their target list, so that at night logically it seemed to us that one might as well keep moving; there was no special protection in waiting until they had passed a certain point, for waiting as we did, say half a mile away, one was just as likely to catch it.

But the sentries posted along the road held to the contrary view.

"*Perkele!*" cried Canada, as we were waved to a halt. The drone above us was certainly ominous, low, intense, thudding and thickening. We had passed the billet and were close by the station, sheltered by insignificant trees. I glanced behind. Our stalwart wounded could be seen to be quietly talking and smoking. I rapped on the window at their cigarettes. They looked at me, and perhaps cupped their mittened hands further about the telltale glow, but otherwise took no notice. "*Jumulant!*" expostulated Canada—God help us, or also and equally, "Dammit." He was positively talkative this evening. Perhaps he too sensed the end of the war, and wanted to strengthen his personal tie with the Lotta before that happened. Afterwards? It could not be foreseen.

A bomb came whistling, and the car was shuddering to the crash of shattered trees nearby. The pull on the windows and doors was palpable. We got out; it was not very sensible—but interesting to see that a Finn and an Englishman acted as with one accord—for a string of bombs was plumbing down and shrapnel alone would cover this area. Canada had got in among the trees, and I had almost joined him, in one of those movements that bridge yards within a split second, when I thought of the man lying on the stretcher; and in the same movement, turned sharply sideways and already extending arms and legs for a jump upwards rather than down, I had reached the back step and joined the wounded and shut the door before the explosion happened. We were smacked over into a heap. The door tore open. The tearing light showed me the Socialist, the Tampere mechanic, lying there, gloomily absorbing every second of it, but he was sweating, sweating profusely, poor devil. The crash and nearby thud were tremendous. For once they appeared to have hit the station.

I used my torch, and mopped his forehead; with the help of one of the sitting cases I eased the position of his legs, then gave him a drink and a cigarette. He was too ill, anyway, to stop me, though his look burgeoned with distrust and dislike of anyone doing anything for him. When I asked him, "What is your name," in Finnish . . . *"Mikä on nimenne?"* he did not reply; nor did any of them, though they were his comrades, offer to give it. They viewed me with the same distrust, taciturnly; though, there again, once they had heard my question in Finnish they began using their language on me in a gruff singsong string of queries. But I didn't understand a word. I had only learned stock phrases.

"Vodka?" one of them said. I knew that.

I shook my head. We had to be going. I took a last look at my principal patient. I was surprised: he was regarding me steadily and thoughtfully. I had come into his line of vision.

From that moment I wanted to know him. What till now had been amorphous in this experience of war and of a northern country, furnished as it was with our civilization but in forms at times so attenuated as to have become ghostly, crystallized at that particular instant into a wish to get to know this man. It was as if, apart from our pacifist witness, I suddenly knew why I was there. Here was a rough, uncompromising fighter, a moralist out of the arctic dark, and though it was extraordinarily conceited of me, with the leaping conceit of twenty-one, I felt that we had principles in common, and enough even of the same nature, to make despite all obvious differences an exchange of ideas worth while. I wanted to know about him; his background, and why Dr. Stromfors should single him out as so important for their country. I wanted him to know about me, out of a much gentler, easier background but who equally over the nub of principle found myself beside him tonight—with still the chance, if a bomb had our names on it, of falling here beside him forever. Perhaps I wanted to justify to someone like this my refusal to be a soldier, to someone for whom moral fervor mattered. And I would have been glad to have made at least one contact that would open up the life of Finland: and it is interesting that when I thought like this a Swedish Finn such as Lars Stromfors, good friend though he was ultimately to become, did not quite qualify. Nor did Canada nor the Légionnaire, because I could not feel their lives in depth. But immediately, tenuous though the outline was, the Tampere mechanic fitted the bill.

But it was a passing notion. There were the difficulties of language, and the conditions of war sweeping you together and apart again in a matter of hours. It was different for those who shared a dugout, or a submarine, or a prison camp, though maybe it was the very ephemerality that gave to my wish an obstinate intensity that, although it was soon to be buried beneath the rush of wartime events, nurtured it through a quarter of a century.

I could not foresee this at the time, of course. I was back at the wheel heading for the hospital, through the starlit night now patchy with mist, mustering my remains of concentration to take the car along the rims of the ruts so as not to jolt those fellows, and so at a certain controlled speed, which speed exasperated Canada, who was crying, *"Huvää! Huvää!"* meaning "Good," on account of the plane-dispelling mist, but whose feet thrust at imaginary accelerators and whose visage shone with sly appetite and a bleak hatred turned on me.

At this point of the journey I had to grin. Our orders were to look in first at the PSP, the Casualty Clearing Station, to leave some cases and take on others. But, once or twice before, and . . . yes, again now, Canada was imperiously gesturing me forward, assuming, so great was his inward agitation, the look of the Vanrikki himself; and he was pointing at the back and miming "Full up!" and this with a look of utter contempt such as townsmen reserve for peasants. For him just then I was equally a peasant; indeed all the world, except for his darling, were clods, peasants, insufferable boors. One had to grin because in looks and smell Canada was the archetypal peasant.

We reached the hospital. I had been conjuring a phrase, in inadequate Finnish, and had it ready. I wanted to say "I am an English Socialist"—at that time true, though not today—and I had produced *"Olen englantilainen sosialisti,"* which seemed to convey it. I wrote this phrase out on paper, and before the orderlies took the stretchers I climbed into the back again and handed it to my Tampere friend.

I was right to think "friend," for before he read it his face resumed its steady stare, as if I had not budged in the interim from him, and after he had read it he nodded weakly, tried to raise his arm, then said distinctly, in a sturdy though failing faraway voice . . . "Pekka Suusanen . . . Tampereelta." Then he actually produced a smile, of solidarity, of recognition, a cautious grayed-over smile; then, as they carried him off, he fainted.

I never thought I should see him again. Pekka Suusanen—when it came to the point, years later, I had forgotten the name until I looked it up in my diary.

The rest of the night continued as usual. We could not stay long at the hospital, with dawn approaching along the road. There were coffee and bread and sweet porridge, and while Canada disappeared to whisper and the Matron came suspiciously prowling, ever watchful of her Lotta brood, I chatted to a fellow ambulance driver who had just arrived from a similar run, who also had news of Äitojoki, where others of our Unit were stationed. We were split in three sections down the eastern front, with the Unit doctor in Sortavala hospital. We heard of one another through notes and chance meetings. For the rest, it was the life of one's own group and the mornings ahead of thick sleep, the uncertain afternoons, and the roomy nights when each minute could be stretched to the full or they'd go by in an oafish daze.

For the most part they were soon forgotten; they had been lived, it was enough.

But that one night, because of what follows, deserves to be remembered.

2

THE SUUSANEN FAMILY IN 1965

WROTE those first pages last week, sitting in this Tampere flat. I wanted to keep the past distinct and the product simply of my wartime diary posted out from England, and of the memories and emotion that rereading set loose. Though as if to help, to make sure I remembered, the day I started a blizzard came up, sweeping the snow with such force against the window it was like an attack of giant sea gulls. Albatross wings clouded out the sky. There was no mistaking the Finnish winter.

Then, half easing the suffocation, the wind plummeted five stories down and lifted the storm with a whirling and a whistling and the scattering, one would have said, of a billion feathers, so that I could see the yard and the slope with its flagpole and the other buildings of this city estate, workaday cubes, each indistinguishable, and beyond them the line of birch beyond which was the misty expanse of frozen lake. People on skis. Traffic on the road. Signs once again in Finnish.

Then back came the wind with annihilating fury, and it was as if, behind the protective glass, I was being rapidly funneled upward to be encaged at the heart of the blizzard.

Next day the wind had gone. There was glittering sunshine. It seemed the end of winter. And although still writing about wartime snow, with its overtones of ghostly horror, I was looking at snow that was fulgent and friendly and crisp and silky to the morning touch. The sun etched patterns on the window; it spilled about the room. Out on the slope children were tobogganing, in their brightly colored quilted anoraks, and a working party of tiny trappers was heading for the lake. Prams were out. Washing fluttered. Balconies shook to the beating of carpets. At the corner shop there was a press of women, decorously stamping their boots as they entered. I joined them, my dictionary flapping—for there seemed to be not a word of Finnish one could guess from any other language—to ask for ground Colombian coffee, and with it a slice of poppy-seed cake. Then I came back to the empty flat, where not even the students were in at that hour, though there were echoes around from the family breakfast, and made Finnish-style coffee in the smaller coffee kettle, making sure it frothed up three times, and had this with the poppy-seed cake. A break for coffee and cake is as Finnish as intrinsically it is Viennese.

But it was only a break—because of the peace and security of the heated flat, and the heartening wash of sun outside, as against the bitter night I was recalling. Half an hour later I was back at this table, back at the wartime JSP. Those memories had to be set down quickly, before the present entered in too much. Already with Lars, as I had seen him occasionally over the years, the portrait must be touched with how I was accustomed to seeing him now—that bit about equality, perhaps; we were equal today, but perhaps in the tent I had been a shade more deferential, he had been more magnanimously superior . . . well, I couldn't be sure.

So, more important, as I had come to Tampere expressly to meet that other person, that intrepid fighter called Pekka Suusanen, who had loomed out of the Karelian night, I did not want him as I found him now to fog up the earlier picture. This was difficult, as I was seeing him daily. It was difficult as he had the personality, backed by such different surroundings, to blot out any trace of the past. So in order to preserve the wartime impression—slight but also useful as a bearing—from the avalanche of the present, I had at least in these hours alone to speed its writing up.

Apart from that, I had to go out to get my one hot meal of the day. Coffee I was able to make in the kitchen, when, of course, the Suusanens weren't there, but anything more might have offended. It was an imprecise subject between us. It was becoming easier, because their daughter, who by now had reached my house in London, had phoned to say that she was allowed to make coffee—those six Finnish cups a day—and was even encouraged to dig about the kitchen for anything she fancied for her supper. Such bohemianism had slightly shocked her, and certainly had shocked her mother.

But it had aided me, and had scotched the idea that I should make my breakfast coffee in my room—on an electric stove, as the students did. I could now breakfast with the family, or at their table, for they had left for work by the time that I got up. There was a place neatly set for me, a cup for coffee and a glass for milk, and a plate for cheese and ham and bread, and an eggcup for an egg if I wanted. The area of liberties was tentatively extended.

But then if I wanted an afternoon snack, and it was amazing how just a glance at the thermometer stimulated the appetite, it was necessary to have bought this while out for lunch, and to eat it direct from the pack-

age in my room. Together with tea brewed on the stove.
It was the only thing to do because at that hour, about
five, the family returned, and the lodgers were expected
to stay out of sight. There were buttery smells coming
from the kitchen, and crockery clatter, and gruff hungry
noises, and splashing from the bathroom, and the scrap-
ing of chairs. All that added to one's hunger, so one had
to have a little food store handy.

Much later, however, after television, to which from
the start I had been formally invited, a family platter
of sandwiches appeared—the open sandwiches or *smörgås*,
by the Finns called *voileipä*—together with tea made with
tea bags, into which one could stir cranberry jam, along
with a dish apiece of *viili*, the thick sour milk eaten with
a spoon. Thus with innate generosity, the cautious peasant sense of measure at this point tossed out of sight,
they kept up with what they had heard their daughter
was receiving in London.

This keeping up, they showed by little signs, was rather
important to them.

So there remained the one hot meal out. (At the weekends, when they were solidly at home from one o'clock
on Saturday, I had so far pushed off to Helsinki.) And
this one meal out meant catching a bus past similar city
housing estates, all of clean, simple design, with open
space between and views to the lake, with district heating, with convenient shops, and with a most refresh-
ingly constant flow of buses and taxis within easy reach.
Beyond were rather smarter flats, put up by cooperative
associations, and the ultramodern church and hospital.
All housing was expensive in Finland. It had been a

key problem ever since the war. Rents were high, rates soared, people preferring to buy their apartments were faced with rising mortgage charges, but in return the buildings and the municipal services were of outstanding quality. The money that was taken was imaginatively spent. It was seemingly the topic with the loudest grumbles, but also with much just satisfaction.

Rounding off this district of housing was the railway line, and after that came the center of the town. Here was the modern plate-glass look in stores and restaurants and towers of flats. There were older buildings of Victorian solidarity, timbered houses and workers' barracks, many of these on the factory estates that were indistinguishably mixed in, and the high brick walls of factories. There were schools, churches, civic establishments, ranging in style from Sonck's cathedral to the latest curvilinear creations that followed the thinking of men like Aalto and Korhonen and Revell. And though this town center was concentrated, there were still trees and a feeling of space, and the promise once snow and ice had gone of green avenues and parks and of the two blue lakes on either side of the city that nonetheless were almost touching.

For Tampere lay on an isthmus, beneath Näsijärvi and Pyhäjärvi (*järvi* being the word for a lake), with power-producing falls as a link; and near these falls one could best see the factories, see how basic they were to the city; and a rooftop view showed more factories continuing along the shores of the lakes, a chain of chimneys rising out of woods; and as one wandered around the streets, there was scarcely an alley without a workshop, then between, say, a block of flats and a row of old timber dwellings would arise yet another formidable factory, but always so clean, so neatly fitted in, that it did not mar the view or the amenities. On the contrary, it could be justly argued that the essential beauty of Tampere city, lakes and woods and hillocks excepted, resided in its being a factory product, an extension throughout the twenty-four hours in shop and home and cafeteria, as if through infinitely extended gearing, of the standard time-and-motion-controlled, welfare-supervised factory bench. So here it was as natural to approve of the factories as in Mecca one would the mosques.

I had been born myself to industrial Bradford, with hooters starting off the day and looms clattering into the night, so I was no stranger to this situation except that the remembered Yorkshire grime, the oppressiveness of its factory landscape, here had been avoided. It pointed one believed to a difference of attitudes, the overhang of the nineteenth century as against one, the Tampere one, already pressing out of the twentieth.

The industrial face of this town was stimulating.

But this was only one factor impinging on those lunch-time hours, when after a meal I went for a walk in and about the heart of the city; other factors seemed to say the opposite.

Well, I began by noting the comparative affluence, the approach to a Swedish or German level, and by thinking how fantastic was this achievement. All the world knew of the challenge—quantities of dead, of widows and orphans, following the two defeats by Russia, in 1940 and 1944. Half a million Karelians to resettle, on land that had to be expropriated, then aided through taxes and capital levies. Reparations to be paid on a scale that involved one-eighth of industrial labor working for Russia for eight years. Lapland to be rebuilt from the ground. All this and more accomplished; Finland, the country that paid its debts . . . that was how Americans understood it. Brave little Finland, outstanding in adversity, a modern David, a Hercules, that had put its trials to such good purpose that today its average standard of living was among the highest in the world.

Well, starting on such trains of thought I naturally thought back to the beginning. I had seen the moment of first defeat and the agonies of the ensuing weeks. Few Finns had conceded defeat, for till then they had fought the Russians to a standstill; but on March 13, 1940, when peace was declared, it only needed another month, with winter yielding to the clarity of spring, for the Russians to come through their defenses. They had nine days to vacate Karelia to the new imposed frontier. First came the soldiers streaming past our billet, an unending stream and straggle of skis and sleighs and horses and heavy lorries, all cut to the same speed, the speed of worn-out infantrymen, heavy-faced, resentful that foreigners should be witnessing this private misfortune. They went past to prepare a new line, and all that summer stayed alert in case the Russians should break the agreement.

Next began the departure of civilians. The sleighs returned seventy to a convoy, aided by buses, lorries, trains, and odd vehicles such as our ambulances, in what by now was a seven-day effort to get the people and their movable goods back behind the safety line. Outside every house still in use, in farms, villages, market towns, there were piles of furniture and trunks and tools to be taken first to the nearest railhead, then by train to a system of depots. As always the organization was meticulous—and remarkable in that it was improvised, coolly and correctly perceived in a flash, and carried through with a hunter's flair. Finns, pushed to the last extremity, were able to keep a grip on reality that, in my experience, Greeks, Poles, Pakistanis, and Arabs were not able to do. The difference lay in their moral perception of the paramountcy of the common need. Any one of them would have been ashamed to betray it.

We worked day and night, shuttling people. Some burned their farms before leaving, some simply locked the door. Where they could not take the cattle, they took parts of the carcass, leaving a bloodily frozen remainder; or there were cows left, lowing with their milk. Nobody had time to milk them. A Swede came through, a volunteer, more vocally distressed than the quiet Finns, and as in some film of the Middle Ages he marched wrathfully from homestead to homestead bashing and smashing anything of value left by the evacuee convoys. In Leppäsyrjä village, or was it Suistamo, for shuttling to and fro we kept on seeing him, he personally devastated the school, even tearing the children's exercise books. Nothing, nothing, to be left for the Russians—*"Ingenting skall lämnas åt ryssarna."*

Well, there weren't many who didn't feel that way.

We retreated to Värtsilä, then to Joensuu. "Black Good

Friday" came, it was over, but the movement of people had to continue from temporary camps and homes
to the interior. The roads were turning from ice to slush,
the routes over the lakes were cracking. The sky was
breaking into pastels, but still with the black envelop-
ing nights; and on one night returning from Kuopio,
perhaps because now one looked at it differently, could
appreciate its cold beauty, we detected to the north the
Aurora Borealis, like a probe of searchlights brighten-
ing until the whole sky had a greenish glow.

Next day (I am copying from my diary) it rained, and
we had some hours off in Joensuu; and whereas people
while in transit were staunch, sometimes cheerful, but
mainly staunch, kind to one another, restrained, all-
enduring—so that one woman, I noted, who had twins
during the journey in the back of the ambulance, set
off from the depot at Kuopio without pause, with a strong
proud walk as if she had evened out the loss, not just
of her family but of all Karelia—in Joensuu the mood
was different. Too many dazed, chilled people were
huddled on public floors and stairways and were milling
round the crowded center of the town. More alcohol
was being consumed (and that is certainly to broach a
topic): more arrack and schnaps and akvavit were being
tossed against desperate furies, the fury of loss, the spirit
of revenge. Morale was high at the first call to action,
but in between, in this refugee center, the mood was
very hurt and violent. That day a man was stabbed badly.
Knives were quickly drawn at that time. Officers on leave
had often the duty of pacifying the street or restaurant
in which they happened to be passing the moment.

Such were the Finns at their lowest ebb. They were defeated again four years later, and again people had to flee from Karelia and again start their world from scratch, but that was near the end of a worldwide conflict from which they were lucky to escape so easily, in view of their recent allegiance to the Nazis. In 1940 they had stood alone. They had been battered unfairly. They had narrowly endured.

So, returning to my walks through Tampere a quarter of a century later, I was obsessed and puzzled by something in their faces. They were not embattled now. They were prosperous and confident. They had actually turned the disasters of war to every form of social progress. Admittedly it was near to the end of winter, and the winter was dark and harsh in the north, but did that explain these malignant faces, more pronounced than anything recalled from 1940? Admittedly here I was in the province of Häme, among the Tavasts, with only some refugee Karelians worked into the local stock; and through all history the men of Häme had been noted as sullen, suspicious, and conservative, and taciturn and earnest and obstinate, with small gray eyes above short stiff bodies (leaving aside more beguiling virtues). But did that justify this utter bleakness, these faces that often looked crushed by stress? Had one to go back across the centuries to peasant forebears who had known hunger, and brutish lives, and constant despoiling? Were such memories stamped on the present—besides which the trials of 1940, my point of comparison, were as nothing?

For I was obsessed and depressed by surly faces, by rancid faces, by unsteady faces on the verge of breakdown into melancholia or some shocking violence. The quality of life-annihilating drunkenness met daily in the street unhinged one; in restaurants there would always be somebody gone that much further than his fellows, but reflecting, as his facade collapsed, their unhappiness taken to its destructive conclusion. They were an unhappy people, they made one sad—and this despite their tremendous valor, and uprightness, and social achievements that, as I say, spoke from every side. I had always thought Yorkshire on a wet Sunday the ultimate in public gloom, but it was Mediterranean beside a walk through Tampere.

There came one afternoon that nearly finished me. There were people in the street, average citizens, looking gray and puritan and buttoned up, not chancing a glance with anyone; and through them came the distraught figures, eyes fixed on arctic horizons; and the stoppers and brooders, the no-longer competent to decide on the value of any direction, and those whose competence kept them wavering in doorways or zigzagging and butting the wall; and on the road itself were the murderous drivers, those whose violence was legitimately unleashed; and after a long wait in order safely to cross on the pedestrian crossing, I escaped as I thought into a restaurant that was also one of the three or four places where one could order a beer or glass of wine without the rigmarole of food.

Disaster. There were several merely tipsy people, averagely locked in gloom and foreboding; there was a Salvation Army girl collecting; there was music, the convenience of excellent cloakrooms, a chucker-out, good

2￼

solid furniture—in fact the most hopeful of northern
settings for a quiet glass and a look at the news. Disaster for me, for the chair opposite was almost at once
taken by a man who decided, as he could not focus
properly, to stare with a mixed contempt and disgust
that wandered about me as though to nail the point
from which my existence sprang. Then this look froze
and he slumped forward, his fall knocking over his
beer. Then, just as one hoped for a rescue party—that
chucker-out with the policeman's eyes—the fellow stood
up, pulled to his feet by some possibly declamatory im-
pulse, and stretched full height, and crashed to the floor.

Everyone stared, with that bleak immobility. I could
see in their eyes that there were areas of blame I could
not possibly conceive of. I felt it was a truly frightening
country.

I would have left there and then, if it hadn't been
for Pekka.

For in Pekka and his wife, and their grown-up children, one came on the other side of the picture. Of
course, Häme people could be lived with. They were
warm-hearted, deeply feeling folk—and this despite the
forbidding exterior, just as grim upon occasion with
Pekka. For seen and only seen in the street, he too
would suggest misanthropy. Seen as I had already seen
him in his cups, he too was shaky with violence. He
habitually looked grim. He was a jowly bulldog. But
seen at home, in the family setting, all this was lit quite
differently.

So already I was content to remain in this town, eager
to do so, to get to know Pekka.

Last night—but no, I had better set down how I came in touch with the family. It was not through Lars, finally. I had written to him from Leningrad, towards the end of a journey in Russia, proposing that as Finland was so near we should not just have another brief encounter, but that I should stay for a month in Helsinki (with Lars, one could write Helsinki, not Helsingfors; for a Swedish Finn, he was advanced in such matters) and travel about—he had a magnificent car, he liked to travel, he was semiretired, and he had often offered this prospect when in London—but alas he replied that he was off to the Canaries for a complete rest. His specialist had insisted. He joked that he might after all be a victim of some obscure Scandinavian malaise, for it was fatigue, world-weariness, introspection that figured as the benumbing symptoms.

But, of course, if I wished I could stay in his flat. He was divorced, but his stepmother lived with him; and she, like all her circle, delighted in getting up parties for friends from abroad. I had better not talk of Leningrad with her, for she only understood it as St. Petersburg, just as Helsinki would only be Helsingfors, and the Finns proper best not referred to. (Lars loved these liberal digs at his family.)

To my further question concerning Tampere and a chance of looking up Pekka Suusanen, he had said why not? His cousins, despite amalgamations and take-overs, still worked as directors in the factory complex that still accommodated "the rebel Suusanen." Though, Suusanen was not so rebellious these days, he had recently become an assistant works manager, a predicament for him, for he had kept the same nature—indeed, at family reunions if he was mentioned (and mentioned he was, for there was something about him, although . . . "like us all" . . . he had failed his early promise) the designation "rebel" was spoken sardonically ("for none of us can fight the real world, can we, at least not as we grow older? I too am finding this"—an obscure remark, for how had Lars fought?).

He added, with his usual imagination, that if I preferred a less assisted approach, then both Suusanen's older son and daughter were working in Helsinki. From the phone book he saw that the daughter's address was in Albertsgatan, at the better end. (Here he wrote it in the Swedish form, adding Albertinkatu in brackets.) He knew nothing about her except that she had contributed to a course of English lessons on the radio. She would certainly be most helpful if I phoned. Or . . . and here one could see him plunging on from habitual ways of thought . . . I could always write to Pekka direct . . . in English, although he wouldn't know English . . . without any intermediate help; like that, who knows, a sort of terrier approach, a bit crude, but who knows, it might reach the man best. The truth was he knew little about Suusanen. In the war, as I had referred to the war, well, then they had all been touched by the visionary. Nowadays, life was prosaic, codified. Finland in fact would soon be as dull as everyone knew Sweden to be.

He returned to some notes on his own dilemmas. Then broke off.

He would be back in May.

But at that time (well, not even now) had I considered staying till May.

(I begin to see; I shall certainly have to.)

I wrote to Suusanen, waiting until I had reached Helsinki before posting the letter. I was in a hotel; this was preferable, as Lars himself could not be my host. I settled to a round of meeting people, on newspapers and in the University, who could give some broad view of their country—differing, needless to say, among themselves as chalk from cheese. Is there such a thing as an objective analysis? Do learned diagnoses and careful statistics connect up to the pulse of a nation, or only, laggardly, to what has crystallized? Conceivably isn't the man in the street, as picked out say by television, who himself is a part of the unrehearsed, untabulated living moment, a more useful guide to one's curiosity? (One can see this more clearly if the country is distant and the man in the street of a different color; then we feel he is as representative as anybody else of that odd kidney.) But of course the instant impression won't do for more than an instant's thought on the matter—but take that man, that television pickup, and work alongside him or live with his family long enough for a thousand impressions or a million to follow each other and ramify; then surely one absorbs through continuing osmosis the real living meat of his life, which is as close as one can get, closer far than generalized and often long-distance essays, to the present pulse of his society. In this case, Finland, 1965.

So I began to think about this possibility while waiting for Pekka Suusanen to reply.

Though, with such slight connection, wouldn't it need an appalling nerve to take things further?

In the event, it needed neither nerve nor guile. It

was enough that the curiosity was genuine. Pekka's elder daughter took charge thereafter.

The call, in both senses the call, came at a polite 10 A.M. A crisp but shakingly vibrant voice phoned to say she was Marjatta Suusanen and delegated to speak for her father. He had been very pleased to receive my letter. He remembered my ambulance, and he wanted me to know that he had recovered very well from his injuries. He had kept a slight limp. He had often wondered what an Englishman had been doing there. Would I by chance have time to visit Tampere? He would like to arrange a dinner for me.

My heart fell at this. A quick advance, but not conceivably on a useful tack.

I hummed and haahed and must have sounded an idiot.

The vibrantly sincere voice forged on; if I knew Helsinki it might be easier if I first met her, at her secondary school. Over their morning break for coffee she would introduce me to her colleagues. They mostly spoke English. (An encouraging laugh.) Could I be so kind as to come?

So I went to the school picturing a maiden of somewhere around twenty-three, slim, positive, and very easy-mannered; and could not at first place the figure who was older, pudgy, more of a boxer build, with features already lined with stress, and with an awkwardness that paralyzed us. Only her eyes, clear and virginal, conformed to the earlier image. Her voice, no longer liberated by the anonymity of the telephone, had receded into a slow neutrality. She wore an excellent suit, of a

serviceable color, and heels a little high for the fashion.
As surprise lapsed, one studied her more carefully.
Over coffee she smoked all the time.

Her colleagues talked, of studies in Brighton, making
it sound like Samarkand, and of years at Columbia and
Berkeley Universities, and of trips to Russia, to match
my own, agreeing that the Russians were a courageous
people but not conceding more than that. The love that
pours from the Russian heart totally seemed to have
passed them by. The erratic brilliance, the inventive-
ness, for them had simply not appeared above the shoddy
public canvas. In sum, they had noted the backwardness
—oh, interesting in Pacific Islanders, but dangerous in
a neighbor so crudely strong! It had to be lived with,
but every feeler going out from Finland to take her
further into the world community of nations went west,
as far west as possible.

All this was said quietly and clearly; no one smiled—
if you tried to make them smile, by way of a joke, they
grew cautious as though slippery ground were approaching; it was a sensible midmorning footnote to the general
interest in public affairs. Miss Suusanen, evenly smoking, occasionally scanning one's soul with her eyes, did
not disagree. At the end she looked gratified by the success of the coffee and conversation.

"I will ring you once again," she promised. As well, as
nothing had been broached about Tampere.

That evening, late, came her telephone voice, at first
vibrantly husky with apology for troubling me at such
an hour. She often couldn't sleep, she volunteered, and
had a passion for detective stories. She had phoned her

father, who was so very keen to meet me; and perhaps I was staying for some time in Finland? Did I require a base in Helsinki? For she herself was leaving for London, a little before the school vacation, on a government-sponsored study scheme. Well, once there, she would take several courses, so as not to waste a minute. So I could have her flat. So she had also been wondering, was there any chance of an exchange? Her flat was very small, she must apologize.

Apologize! I was completely floored by the fluency of her proposition, coming as I now knew it to do from a shy and circumspect woman. The phone was quivering with overexcitement, with life-mastering optimism.

Cautious in turn, I asked to see the flat, wondering if she would say, come now.

But the call came for the following day, at teatime, for coffee and cakes.

She answered the first press of the bell, her face strained with indecision. She only reluctantly let me in. She sat at the far side of the room, anxious about the space between us, and very gravely heard out the praise that a first view of her flat called for. Again surprise, for it was a model flat (my thought, not bad for such a man's daughter), with low chaste lighting and chaste birch chairs, leather-backed, on a vinyl flooring, and all of this so swept and polished one could not believe that anyone used it, and lithographs, with a leaning to the abstract, and neatly tucked away, tape-recorder, and television, and radiogram. Along one wall were mostly English books, and the cooking facilities boxed into the other. Beyond was the bathroom, then presumably

the bedroom. "May I have a look?" It was the purpose of
the visit. She showed me the bathroom but left me alone
to see, if I really had to, the bedroom. As I rejoined her
she said, "I am a little stiff. I am sorry, I do not make
friends easily." Shakingly lighting a cigarette she motioned me to the table for coffee.

She continued to apologize for half an hour. She
slowly added subject to subject, such as her inability to
cook (apropos of no homemade cakes), the weather, her
continuing defects in English, the possibility that the
Government would be wasting money in sending her
to London. She was not interested in any other view. Talk
of an exchange of flats was suspended. I approached it
along another tack, by saying I should like to stay in
Tampere; but at the time this did not seem to register.
There were moments of utter emptiness between us as
trails of conversation ended. There was a neatness about
her features then only otherwise to be seen in chapel.
She bowed before existence, as though in penance—then
suddenly she was saying, "I am afraid, I have been working so hard all winter I have not until now had a chance
to be spontaneous. I am so glad of this opportunity."

In fact, she was somehow enjoying herself!

Very quickly thereafter we reached agreement; for
she had understood my cue about Tampere and had
conscientiously in the meantime solved it. She had the
solution ready in her mind. In return for accommodation
in London, she would ask her parents if I could stay with
them (they already let one room to students; and I could
converse, at least with her mother, in Swedish), and her
flat here would go to a colleague, and at a rent that

would pay her parents for me. Thus absolute fairness would be observed; and in addition, she knew, her father would thank her for bringing an old comrade to his door.

We did not bother further with details. (Later I was to write my wife to spoil her, a gesture that caused her to phone from London and insist on her parents spoiling me.) And as well we did not, for her enthusiasm, perhaps only made possible face to face by the impetus of an accelerating mind, was already quietening. Doubts had set in. How could an arrangement that was perfect for her be quite so good for the other party? She had spoken hastily. I had to forgive her.

Alas, suddenly she was certain I didn't want it, that I was being polite, that she was only a nuisance. She told me, sincerely, that she was very selfish.

It seemed the moment to slide away, to leave things to the telephone.

Sure enough, again at an advanced hour, with an almost flighty burst of greeting now perhaps that I had been to her flat, came her other-personality voice, full of certainty, of revelation, informing me that all had been arranged. No word concerning her parents' feelings at the prospect of a lodger who couldn't speak Finnish, no more than I had warned my wife; it was a moment of pure telephonic freedom, a giddiness born of the instrument itself. She ended by mentioning the thriller she was starting, as sleep was now impossible. . . . I suppose, wanting to share it a little.

I saw her once again before she left for England, at the air terminal, looking very pale, very uncertain, very contrite, so recessive in fact that she barely noticed the double whiskies I was ordering for her and which she took like sips of water. It was good to see the glow on her cheeks, despite herself, coming through. She was saying she would send a postcard on arrival.

Helsinki, to be truthful, is small beer after the splendors of Leningrad. It has its charm and curiosity, but like Stockholm it is more of a summer capital, with endless sorties possible then to the chain of islands and island waters stringing outward from its harbors. In winter, for all its cosiness and a certain crankiness, it is insipid. Finns, of course, crowding into it as they do from every corner of their country, find it a very heady place, and it does have some international luster, and it does produce the most beautiful objects in glass and wood and metal and fabrics, and its commentary on the rest of the world, indirectly most interesting in theatrical production, has an athletically moral fervor (that fellow-worshipping Sweden has dropped, or in Sweden perhaps the fervor is decadent), but for all that it is a workers' capital—oh, of highly educated, self-respecting workers set up a vast number of them now as bureaucrats, who are full of weighty progressive schemes activated by a Lutheran conscience (and in saying workers one equally means yeomen, for the Finnish peasant was always technically free; and as for the older ruling class, it is being squeezed and tamed and absorbed by the aftereffects of war and taxation)—and so one gives all praise for this achievement—which if they want it is more of a light to the emerging nations than, for instance, is Moscow—but, this said, it remains insipid.

So, from this aspect, Tampere could be worse.

But not at all, for Tampere is industrial, historically the Red city, the bastion of the emerging worker, and for all the creeping veneer of the capital a coarser punchiness remains. Hooters, the whirr of machinery, the smells, that thick tanning smell near the rapids, fix what Tampere is without pretense. Coming from Helsinki one looks for less, and suddenly finds one is given more, and straighter, aimed at the solar plexus. A thought that would gladden certain fellow Bradfordians, who spurn the more rarefied London air. In addition Tampere is edged by lakes and woods that are equally part of it in winter; at Pekka's factory, for instance, at lunchtime, the workers are out on the ice, skating. There is a virile mood, a generosity; Tampere in many fields is leader.

And I don't, writing this, forget the schizophrenia.

It is time to get things down to Pekka. I begin to see, he stands for so much of it.

Last night, the wartime pages finished, I was looking forward to his company. It was the family sauna evening and he, together with Martta his wife, took the lift down to the basement sauna, which is reserved for them for an hour each Wednesday. On Saturday he may have another sauna, a more sociable one with men from the factory, or his Union friends; and there are other kinds of sauna for special celebrations, for welcoming a guest, for meditation, for settling disagreement—many uses of the sauna. But on Wednesdays it was a prelude to a change of linen and a quite amicable family evening. So it was an honor, a treat, if he also invited his lodgers to join him after his supper. A manifestation of very deep good will.

Shortly after he had gone to the sauna I knocked on the door of the students' room. Their room, like mine, led off the hall, and opposite to us were bathroom and kitchen; then beyond them was the parental bedroom, leading out of the sitting room. Their room had belonged to the daughters, Marjatta and Helmi, Helmi being married and living nearby; my room had belonged to the sons, to Olavi, who was married and working in Helsinki but to whom Marjatta had not referred, and to Aarne, now a boy of nineteen years, who since my arrival had slept on the settee in the sitting room and who didn't seem to mind this. One could be sure he didn't mind, for he was excessively good-natured, illogical and mad, and a jazz fanatic, very much a part of his generation and so up against that of his father. He too was starting off as a mechanic, but he had already changed his firm twice, allegedly for better training schemes. But he was not a rebel; one had only to look at him, while his still-battling, still-wrestling-with-it father had stayed with the one firm all his life.

But more later about Aarne, for he had many sides, and he was very much on Pekka's mind. He had some words of English, and quite a bit of Swedish (though he was not interested in taking that further), and in any case he communicated, and could have done in any part of the world, through his string-it-along, keep-it-moving nature.

I knocked on the girls' door. They said, "Hello? Mr. Sykes? You may come in." They both spoke a high, uninflected English, like two little birds in their students' cage. Much younger than Marjatta, their shyness was different; with them it was a product of impossible good

manners combined with an avid need to observe. They
were studying to be journalists, at the School of Social Sciences, and they felt that nothing should miss
their attention. They were experts on the Suusanen family, so potentially invaluable aides for me, though there
their sense of correctness intervened, and some embryonic
professional secrecy, so they spilled as little of the truth
as they could. They saw me as another bit of news, to be
sifted and checked, though because of their upbringing
they had difficulty in doing more than look; then afterwards, a miniature newsroom at work, one could hear
them twittering and dropping pencils and finally typing
out a conclusion. Coffee in their room—they had an electric kettle, and a stove for cooking on-the-job snacks—
was an intense, often silent, invigilation.

You have to get used to silence in Finland.

It is a major part of social communion.

"Mr. Sykes," they seemed more relaxed this evening,
"can you please define for us a gentleman?"

"Don't you have a word for him in Finnish? At a guess,
from the Swedish? Herra-something? Suggesting who
was once lord of the manor?"

Oh dear. They looked stuck, with palely smiling puz-
zlement. What to do with an indelicate topic? They were
both large girls, tall, blonde, with fat country cheeks and
thighs. Not thinking, the one who came from Haapamäki reached for a cigarette—to realize she must have
tucked them away the moment they had heard my knock.
Mrs. Suusanen disapproved of girls smoking, and these
girls, whom one could always hear striking matches, an
essential part of their chosen career, went to all lengths

to dispel the fumes—warming up pasties, opening the double window, working the door into the hall. I at once offered her one of mine. "Between writers. Between students. It helps to concentrate." "Oh no, we couldn't. It is not allowed." "I know, but at times one simply has to." Aghast (it seemed) at such breach of convention, eyes wide open to what it might lead to, they instituted a lengthy pause; then, unexpectedly, helped themselves.

They didn't, however, reveal their own store.

But they were not mean; they offered biscuits and coffee. And now, a tremendous hurdle surmounted, talk more easily found its way. They didn't always know what to do with their legs, or with a smile if it reached the lips, but topic for topic, trade for trade, they opened out of their usual circumspection. I told the one who was going to Chelsea, as a summer au pair, the sort of thing to expect; and to the other, much exercised by Africa but unable to visualize a black man, how quickly this facet of color faded; and in return they told me that Mrs. Suusanen, who looked so composed, so solid, so soothing —and who was certainly the one with a spark of humor— also suffered from terrible headaches and that these derived from the strain of bearing her husband's dislike of the Lutheran Church. Oh yes, this was a tremendous factor! They goggled at my ignorance. I must understand the Church, to understand the Finns. Why, as children, almost wherever they were going, they had been told by their mothers—"Behave as if in church!" The whole of Finland in a diffused sense, now that there wasn't much actual churchgoing, was a church.

"Every man, so to speak, his own pastor?"

"Oh yes, we worry terribly much about behavior." They giggled, aware of the sinful moment, smoking, and spilling the beans to a stranger.

"So Mrs. Suusanen is a keen churchgoer? Every Sunday?"

"Sometimes. It is difficult for her. He is really deeply hating the Church. We understand it. It is part of his experience. And he has a sister, who married a White farmer, and she is even an active Revivalist; and he refuses to know her. Oh yes. . . ."

"That's interesting. Does she live near here?"

"At Toijala, towards Hämeenlinna. In summer you will see it from the Silver Line boat. You can also go by boat to Virrat, along the Poet's Way. That is near to Haapamäki. I am sorry that I shall be in Chelsea."

"Yes," said the other, "you can see much of Finland, on the old steamboats, by our lake system. The most beautiful excursions for a visitor here. From Kuopio, to Joensuu, to Savonlinna, to Lappeenranta. You eat and sleep on the boat. There is wildlife round you."

"I certainly must do it." My memories of that area were less idyllic. "But how did Mr. Suusanen come to hate the Church?"

"Oh, that is very difficult for us. We did not observe." A laugh. "We were not born." A further pause. It was the end of the session. They were in full retreat.

I thanked them for the coffee and left without dallying. From the farewell silence one could not know whether they remained allies or not.

No twittering or touch-typing followed; almost at once they went out of the flat.

The hour had passed; the sauna was over. The Suusanens, red-faced and doughy, had returned and for a
time were taking it easy. Pekka had switched on the news
and turned it off. There was the gurgle of beer into a
glass. In a home where alcohol was rarely taken except
at selected ritual feasts, an after-sauna beer was permitted; and its pouring out after days of abstinence
was like the song of a waterfall.

Mrs. Suusanen had prepared supper immediately on
return from work, and now only had to take it from
the oven. There had been onion smells and the bubbling
of potatoes, but otherwise not much preparation. Indeed
during the week she had little time after leaving her
factory at four, then shopping (smartly, as the shops closed
at five, making for queues of worker-shoppers), then
catching a bus across the center of town, before Pekka,
fortunately often detained at his factory for consulta-
tions, arrived at the door, hungry. He occasionally got
a leg of lamb or mutton, but usually quick-fried pork
with onions, or meatballs, or some sprat concoction; and
most usual of all were the *laatikko* dishes, which were
simply packets of frozen food. His favorites here, as
could be seen from remains or from the deep-freeze com-
partment of the refrigerator, or from the boxes lying in
the kitchen bin, were the macaroni packet and the minced
liver packet; and of these perhaps the liver came first,
served with boiled rice and maple syrup and a generous
helping of melted butter. Tonight it was certainly a
laatikko dish, with the onions perhaps for a mushroom
entree, with boiled or mashed potatoes (leftovers that,
thriftily tucked into the refrigerator, would be used for

salad with egg and vinegar); and after all that, all easily prepared, together with a tumbler or two of milk, would come the inevitable sweet porridge, or berry soup, or dried fruits and cream. If Aarne was late home, and I had already joined them for the ceremonial television, this was the sort of supper he would get, eating it unobtrusively in the background, his mother mainly attending to him, while Pekka and I, and often the students, side by side faced the screen.

It was the moment of the evening for me when I was called to join them opposite the telly-box.

This evening after the sauna they were resting, eating more slowly, not talking much. For some days past there had been strenuous conversation, some topic that was uniquely engrossing them, that left through the rest of the evening a preoccupied look upon their faces. I could hear them, without understanding the words; though, it's a curious thing living with people whose primary language you can't follow, you develop, as perhaps blind people do, a great awareness of pitch and tone and repetition of certain motifs, so that in a flash you know "they are on to it again, the subject that involves the word *'periaate'* on a variety of forms, what with all those cases— *'periaatteesta,'* isn't is, quite often?" And you follow then, by the alternation of silence and sturdy reiteration, the progress or nonprogress emotionally of the theme in dispute. Not that Mrs. Suusanen tackled him with any complaint or scorn in her voice; she was gentle and patient and even-toned, and she did a lot of listening to him, and then she quietly restated her views. There was a ponderously accepted impasse. The students, I knew, were attending to it also, but here they would not spill a bean. Pekka himself looked tough and worried, and he sounded solemn and challenged and determined not to be rushed into anything new; and he too listened respectfully, then suddenly there might come a flow of words from him, but otherwise it was slow and difficult, and calm and sturdy—but then this was Pekka in every conversation. He was wholly himself all the time.

(Had he changed to look at? Well, I had recognized him, and marked the limp and the scarred hand. He was older, obviously; he seemed rather sedate . . . otherwise, well, already it was impossible to separate out any earlier figure. I had the wartime comment, especially Lars's words—a good thing I had got them down—but though they gave a few rough criteria, any present attempt to measure him to them somehow with him in the room failed. Pekka as he was now absorbed one. And he was hung up on some immediate problem.)

This evening, after the visit to the sauna, there was for a change a benevolent hush. His *laatikko* dish made him smack his lips. There were soothing murmurs about this and that. He was not opening a second beer, but repeatedly they were pouring out milk from the big family jug on the table. She was saying something about her factory—*tehtaassa* . . . in the factory—and mentioning some of her girls by name. She was in charge of the training of seamstresses up to the required factory standard; one evening she had shown me the cards she used with headings such as Carefulness, Ability to Learn, General Conduct, Defects. One could surmise how patient she was, and understanding, and absolutely honest as to whether a girl qualified or not; and conversing in Swedish, which she had learned from her mother and passed on to her children but had otherwise little occasion to use (but even so, it was charitable of her to listen to my performance with it), I had learned more of Pekka's promotion and a little about his factory past. They both worked for the same combine, and for years it had been within the same mill, till he had been sent as an assistant manager to the new plant on the lakeshore. This promotion had very much surprised him, and was not as yet fully digested. Shrugs accompanied her reference to it. As she realized I wanted to get to know him, because of that Winter War encounter, she had fed me a few preliminary details as though to underpin what would come out later. Thrifty, and cautious about the line delimiting the lodger's place, and at moments both reticent and suspicious, she was also instinctively motherly to strangers. As soon as an agreed favor came round, such as joining them for television, she seized the chance to spoil one through it. Tea and sandwiches, and more sandwiches; the more one took, the more approval she beamed.

She was knocking on the door. It was the moment to join them.

What followed actually was rather disappointing; it was not to prove a good evening with Pekka. The students' absence robbed us of interpreters, for he declined to rely on his wife's use of Swedish. He did know a few words of English, and there were signs that he wished to learn it systematically. Both his elder children, Olavi and Marjatta, had shone in English in the course of their studies, and the youngster Aarne seemed capable of picking it up as an adjunct to jazz. So why shouldn't he learn the tongue of the two great nations friendly to his country, or . . . would it in some way mark a betrayal of what he had always stood for in life? For "wasn't it the language of archcapitalism?" he had challenged through the students. I had countered: and also of poets and moralists, in each century of teachers and reformers? Did he blame a language for universal greed? He had climbed down there, but it had revealed his source of worry. He was excessively cautious, it seemed, these days lest he compromise his essential self, put a stout workingman's foot wrong, in a world that was changing just a shade too rapidly. He was ponderously suspicious of innovation. His broad, stocky frame sat there, muscular and swift but disinclined to move, his resolute face looking noncommittal. One could see that, decided, he could move powerfully, possibly with a lightning effectiveness; but he was in a phase of shelving decisions. He just sat, watching you, listening, brooding, as likely to temporize with no as yes. He was a rock of a man (one didn't have to know about his past to see him as that), and one determined only to move in keeping with the deepest morality, that in this phase eluded him slightly. Overall, one sensed his modesty.

This evening he was tired. We watched television. He stared without comment at the craggy faces, craggy as his own, and sober and disciplined who stared at us as they discussed the news. There was a girl singer with a deep rough voice, and wan, flabby cheeks. There was the Lucy Show. Advertisements sold us washing powders, razor blades, cups of chocolate; and there was an item asking motorists please to learn what pedestrian crossings were for. He grunted once, but otherwise was silent. After the sauna and his supper he had lost all his usual questing pugnacity. I was thinking how extraordinary that we were sitting there at all, glued respectfully to television, and that probably in a hundred or more countries that evening a visitor would be similarly entertained; and indeed that if Kinglake had been alive now he too, squatting with his Arabs, would first have had to watch their favorite serial before getting to know them more intimately, for this was today's introduction to the average family anywhere.

Mrs. Suusanen brought tea and sandwiches. A near-silent partaking.

Handshakes. Then bed.

3

FACTORY BACKGROUND

THE household awoke early in the morning. The daily paper was regularly delivered, with a smack as it came through the letterbox onto the polished hall floor, at about four-thirty. At five they stirred. By six they were having eggs and coffee, and open sandwiches of sausage or cheese, together with tall glasses of milk and sometimes *piima,* the curdled milk. Aarne was the last into the bathroom, gasping under the cold shower. Few words passed. There was no music, no commentary from the radio. The austere hour was austerely met, and after a good breakfast they departed.

I only once made the error of getting up, but then observed that Mrs. Suusanen prepared for each of them a thermos of coffee and a packet apiece of assorted sandwiches. She got up first to accomplish this, as they left the flat at six-thirty. The parents each queued for a bus, the son mounted his motorcycle. One saw them in the yard, from the bedroom window—she as always quiet before life, hurrying a step after her husband, who set off with determination. Aarne went past, with a quarter raise of the hand. They continued, silent, to the bus stop.

The road streamed with cars and bicycles, and mud spattering out from the wheels.

On the stroke of seven, hooters sounded.

After their departure it seemed unworthy to continue lying in bed. In a land of lotus-eaters one can do it, but not when living with disciplined workers. There was a two-hour wait for the post. There was a bitter wind blowing most days, with abrupt furious spattering of rain. Neither bed nor the prospect of a walk pleased, so there was nothing for it but to coach oneself with something suitably rigorous, such as Finnish, or a tome on Finnish history, or, found on Olavi's shelves, the *Famous Speeches of American Presidents*. Marjatta also, on leaving home, had left her current thrillers behind her, the Christies and Carrs of the late fifties, but these did not go with the hour. She had additionally been a student of German, so there was an offering of Mann and the plays of Hauptmann, and a Goethe she must have sold to Olavi, for her name had been crossed through and his substituted. Each of their books recorded its owner. There was not a title with Helmi written in. Aarne had mostly books on engineering; Olavi on history, in various languages; and Marjatta, apart from the few books in German, an immense collection of mystery and adventure. I began to picture her combing London for works she had not yet read, to discard them night by night in our guest room, the husks of her insatiable appetite. The postcards she sent—of Buckingham Palace, of Tower Bridge, of the Serpentine—spoke only of legitimate studies, saying, "I am working very hard all the time."

I had read these to Pekka. The students had translated them. He had held them in his hand approvingly.

One could see: in London, or the far corners of the earth, Marjatta would awake at the inner hooter and apply herself to the inbred day. Would come up trumps in the family style. And then get drunk on crime in the evening.

One effect of her postcards and phone calls had been that her mother had pressed me to stay also at the weekends if I wished, and to eat with them on Saturday and

Sunday; and on the second weekend when this was happening, Pekka said, "You want . . . see my factory?" It
was late Friday evening, and after television, after Robin
Hood and the Danny Kaye Show, I had been helping
him for an hour with English. We used a direct reader,
with pictures and phrases thrown inconsequentially at
us, and one of them was "Do you want to see the room?"
"You want . . . see the room?" Pekka struggled; then out
of the blue, "You want . . . see my factory?"

And so it was arranged for the following morning.

I took the bus and arrived at twelve. The ice on the
lake was breaking up, with dirty floes among the reeds,
and black water further out. The woods backed by a
hill at this point were wet with rocks and undergrowth
from which the snow had all departed; the spring sun
glinted off the birch. In the shops they were selling wil-
low catkin, and from the bus I had seen a magpie busy.
It was an intermediate sort of morning, with winter chill
still in the shadows, but giving one soft pause in the sun
so that one stood and looked at the gleaming factory,
built low to the lake and the hill in successive levels, or
promenades—for it could equally have been a thermal
establishment—and felt that it enhanced its setting, that
it dramatized the woods and water.

Not a minute longer; the Finns were punctilious; I
asked for Mr. Suusanen. The gatekeeper phoned, then
sent me over to the office block. An ash blonde, very fluent
in English, added my coat to the coat-hanger rack. She
glanced at my shoes. "Did you come by car?" She had a
way of suggesting this was more than a formula. Then,
dismissing me to an easy chair, she got lost in an office

conversation, in Swedish, about her chances in a lottery. Then again she was leading me, and emphasizing how very tidy she looked from behind, to a door with an array of colored buttons; she pressed the green and a light responded. "So Goodbye"—presumably as I hadn't a car; then she was speaking in Finnish as she handed me over.

She hadn't handed me over to Pekka. For a second I feared I was meeting a Stromfors, one of those several cousins of Lars, a linking up that wouldn't do at this moment.

But . . . "Koivaara—I am the PRO" . . . and a sporty handgrip closed about mine. The glazed feeling induced by offices thickened about us. We both sat back. On one wall there was a shelf of trophies, on two others graphs and stickers showing the relation of production to welfare, and on the fourth a gigantic picture window that seemed actually to enlarge the lake, and to float us into the air above it. "Please take a look." He offered cigarettes, and found it necessary to dial Helsinki; then a buzzer sounded, he pressed a button, and once again the ash blonde appeared, this time in a nylon overall, for she was carrying a tray with coffee on it, rather as if for a theater audition. It was an awful pity I hadn't a car, for like this her cues were wasted. She persisted with her export-conscious smile.

"Please study this at your convenience." He was handing over a beautiful brochure that summed up the Company's achievements. He poured the coffee, and gulped his down. "And now I think we must start our tour. Which

aspect of our production in particular . . . are you
. . . ?" Smugly, "We have no secrets."

"Er—well, you see, through Mr. Suusanen——"

"Yes, yes, he is waiting." He was suddenly brisk, checking by his watch, and leading to the corridor. "We shall
see him in the factory. It has been arranged. But for
visitors, my office . . . has the honor . . . please." He was
indicating that we should climb some stairs. He was already at the top. He was in good trim. "I will show you
first the recreation rooms—these are the ones for office
employees. You see—piano . . . discussion room . . .
and here the hair shop . . . here changing rooms." He
swung open a door. Another ash blonde stood staring at
herself in a mirror. "Oh, excuse." She smiled sweetly. We
turned about, to be caught by another picture window.

He used it to show the factory layout. Carding, spinning, weaving sheds, the scouring and dye house, the
finishing plant—and he asked me not to believe those
people who said the lake was being polluted; a superior
process was now in use. And here (we were skating away
down a passage, skimming down steps, nodding at people) were more clubrooms, and the main canteen. Had
I imagined that such facilities were only for the office
staff? No, no, the best was available for all. Here, look,
at special Company prices were hot lunches and cold
lunches that had been worked out by a dietician; and
there was a separate room for "women only," and "self-
provision eating rooms," with refrigerators and hot ovens,
where employees could stack their own-provided food to
find it, hot or cold, in the lunch hour. Showers, lava-

tories, changing rooms. In the lavatories there were black-boards and chalk, for those who felt the urge to write words; and cleaners, of course, to erase the words. For recreation, a variety of courses . . . in home cooking, baby care, orchestration, chess, civics; and an equal variety of sports arrangements. "You see we work for a happy people—in the broadest sense, for a happy Finnish people. The Company is firstly patriotic. Humanity requires more than bread."

This PRO was in his element.

He was now heading across an open space to the poly-clinic and daytime crèche, expounding on pensions and national insurance as supplemented by Company schemes. I had not been slowing him down with questions, because I was getting nervous about Pekka. In half an hour the hooter would go, then what became of Pekka's invitation? Was this the only form it could take? I suspected this official of crowding him out; one caught the whiff of departmental jealousy. We were already beyond the manufacturing sheds.

"Er, Mr. Suusanen . . . ?" I began.

"Yes, certainly. He awaits." He checked with his watch. "On every tour we try to reach each point exactly to the minute. It has been timed for many types of occasion; but if we lose, or gain, we can be flexible. So, please, here is the nurse awaiting us. Then, afterwards . . ." My unease was penetrating. "I will telephone from here to Suusanen."

Watched by a nurse in a bright little surgery, with an even more stunning view of the lake—so that we seemed at this point to be breaking away in a dream sequence across the waters . . . he was drowning . . . the nurse and I, her hair turning to an ash blonde color, were canoeing toward a distant boat house—Koivaara phoned Suusanen. "He awaits." Something of Pekka's mood was conveyed by the sudden drawing in of his mouth. "He will join us now at the training school." We shook hands with the nurse (could she sense my fantasies, was she used to them from the succession of visitors?) and continued to the jetty from which in summer Company boats made the trip to an island, to an all-employee beach and sauna. "You have a camera with you?" He glanced at my pockets.

"I am sorry, no." I was always forgetting it. I could see he was surprised, being used to Germans and Americans who nowadays flipped out a camera as readily as a nail file. (He was right, of course. The visual record. More pat than all these cumbersome words. Though I probably kept on forgetting the instrument because I still hankered after words, their use for shading in memories and so on.) "I suppose the ice will soon have gone?"

"Yes, it will have gone." His tone was flat. He looked let down about the camera.

But we sped on, and to cheer him up I thought of a question to do with strikes. Yes, and how big was the Communist cell? Did Communists set the pace for wages?

No, he replied, facing up to this one, and appreciating that at last I had put a question, the Stromfors Company did not have strikes. Strikes were a rare event in Finland. For, following the cost of living index, wages and other related benefits were settled in central discussions in Helsinki, between the employers and the Unions. Where dispute arose and could not be settled, the government quickly stepped in. Contracts made were not broken. So, generally, no wildcat strikes.

I looked impressed. Did the Communists behave? What role did they play in a factory like this?

He consulted his watch. "I should like to explain this. I see that you know we have a Communist problem. All Finns give it serious attention." He slid a pace on, still hesitating. "Perhaps, a little later, if we take a car, I shall explain. Meanwhile, the schedule . . ." He looked covered, affable, then guarded as the grave as we strode up to Pekka.

The assistant works manager was viewing us stonily. It was difficult to think that he was simply angry, for he must be used to this sort of treatment—except that, of course, I was his guest. Perhaps the first he had invited to the factory. He too was consulting his watch.

But more than this, more than vexed, he looked solemn, solemnly seized by his moment of authority, as though we had been masonic novices and he the one bringing us into the lodge. He waved us into line behind him. Masonic gravity and care for the word, for the proper pace and pause and gesture, ruled his bearing and in consequence ours for the next half hour or so. He let us know we were in his domain. One wondered indeed where was the rebel, the rebel against this system and its masters? Whatever he had been, once upon a time, Pekka now moved like a master. One's reaction was "and it suits him too!"

He didn't acknowledge me as his lodger and evening companion, he kept a formal distance, and from time to time gave a little address, possibly the one he always gave concerning the combined lap-forming unit, and the points in favor of ring spinning, and the difference between Dobby and Jacquard looms. Most of this took place in passages, as we swung from one shed to the next, for against the sustained whirr of machinery, the high hum and clatter and shake, if you couldn't lip-read you couldn't converse, and translation was even more of a strain.

Also, he had his eye on the operatives while we were close up to the machines, watching what they were doing with their fingers, checking their cards, and bins, and waste. Though there were not too many people to watch, the latest machinery was automatic, and shed after shed whirred and gleamed, in color schemes of white and silver and the sun exploding through the long lake windows, with only a few neat women and an occasional mechanic gliding or standing as if already in Elysian groves. It was a dreamlike place (it was if one remembered a sooty Bradford mill in winter) and its guardian was Pekka, or its assistant guardian, for the principal manager was an engineer with a studious face and an armful of samples. It was not what one had visualized —in constructing an image of Pekka's past. But then, it was their latest factory; others in the group were more old-fashioned. It was in one of those he had fought his battles.

He was on top of the job. He had earned his place. This wasn't at all how one had expected to see him— through always thinking in moral terms.

Anyway, how had it come about?

(One simply had to know more about Pekka.)

Meanwhile Koivaara was behaving. He managed to look as though he too were learning (although, it must be for the thousandth time), and that here were good finds for his graphs. Yet, translating, he also managed to imply his set reservations with regard to Suusanen. Too more different men could not have walked together. Pekka was heavily involved with his surroundings—spindles and looms and those who worked them checked and ordered like his own mind and body. While for Koivaara this factory or another was clearly a step toward further peaks. His attitude was superficial, however sharp or smooth it flowed. He kept saying, "But the Company also has the view" . . . trying to cut Pekka to size.

Pekka, if he followed this note, just ignored it.

He spoke to Koivaara without ever quite facing him, then stumped on to the next exhibit.

We were in the finishing department when the hooter sounded, halted before a two-bowl calender as used for tubular knitted fabrics, and here with a variety of short processes there were more women, more girls, some of them basically rather striking with Mongolian and Nordic features, though these were generally overlaid with current pop star characteristics. As the hooter went, the clattering ceased, and silence supervened, in which the sudden rush of voices at first was no louder than a whisper. Pekka moved away for a word here and there. He looked concerned to see they got away quickly, now that their week's work was finished. His smile was paternal, almost romantically involved with these, his soul companions. One got a glimpse of how he held their respect, this manager come up from the ranks—with no question at all of his being a renegade; on the contrary he was an acceptable father figure, one they could at least understand. He limped a bit more as his gait became casual. It was the most homely view I had had of him yet.

Koivaara said, "I fear we have failed to complete our tour on time." He was scribbling a note and tapping his pockets, obviously itching to get away.

"I will thank him," he continued, "and then I will take you, as promised, by car, to see some housing. The car already awaits at the office."

"Isn't that breaking into your weekend?"

"No. For the Company I am always on duty. Later I will referee for the football. This evening, more plans. I work also for the Church. Last year I took our Church youth to England, to Devonshire, to a camp near Exeter."

"That was a long way for you to go."

"Not at all. For also, for the Company, I have accompanied long-service employees to Majorca. After twenty years' service we give each employee a choice of cash or holiday award. That is one of the tasks of my office."

"Has Mr. Suusanen taken such a holiday?"

"No." A faint acerbity returned. "So far he has not accepted an award. He is really our only failure in this. The Company is always seeking to give it. Perhaps . . . perhaps now we shall succeed, for I have been authorized to offer him land, on which he could build his own house. It is Company policy. I will show, by car. Oh look, see, we can thank him at last. . . ."

Pekka was returning. I said hastily, "Mr. Koivaara, excuse me, but I am his guest. I think he should come along with us now."

Koivaara brushed me into silence, then a second or so later fully understood, and momentarily was flattened by such conflicting impossibilities. He began, "He would not wish . . . I fear . . . irregular"; but then, just in time, another thought struck him, and abruptly he was very much on his toes. His manner to Pekka was suddenly most charming.

Pekka naturally reacted suspiciously. They talked away in gloomy Finnish, chill and soft notes alternating. They argued for a moment, then Pekka looked at me, the first time that morning he had looked at me squarely but not even now with much recognition, more in compliance with necessary evil lest more awkwardness befall. He nodded shortly. We stumped to his office. He changed out of his mill coat. On the table were rough heaps of papers, thumbed and mixed; the slide rule was dusty. He was obviously not a paper man. Koivaara sniffed and looked away. Yet this small office breathed decision.

Some minutes later we were seated in a car, a black chauffeur-driven Austin. The chauffeur wore a lumber jacket, and was on gruff familiar terms with both of them. Koivaara did the talking. To me he said, "I am explaining to my colleagues that more than ever the Company stakes its future on welfare. And in welfare, the number one project is housing." He appeared to repeat this again in Finnish. The other two looked unimpressed.

We drove along the lake. It was decidedly pleasant to be sitting in a car and whooshing through the landscape. But Koivaara had things for one to see. First came a block of leasehold flats for the higher grades of administrative employee, that was cut to the same style as the factory, with carports and a sculptured garden and motor launches out on the beach being painted ready for the first days of cruising. Behind this was a block of flats for unmarried office girls—perhaps useful for parties (he didn't say so), as next came an exclusive promontory with villas for the Company directors. One visualized those card-party evenings.

All this was a preliminary through which we sped, as it wasn't the main arm of Welfare. Koivaara said, "From this point on, we approach the workers' own-home area. This is the Company's proudest achievement. A man likes to own his house." Once again he underlined his point in Finnish, smoothly, looking away from Pekka. Though Pekka in turn was staring somewhere else, somewhere indescribably distant, with just the faintest secret humor on his lips.

Koivaara continued, "First is the area of own-home, but Company land. Shall we stop? Will you see? These two-story houses have all been built by their worker-owners. It is good work, I believe." It certainly was. Any visitor would be impressed. The houses looked professionally built, solid, suburban, with three-scaped gardens, and a sauna among the trees or in the basement. Naturally, every house had a sauna. "In the summer evenings, you see, there is time. The Company brings electricity and plumbing, and has an architect to clear the plans. Much of the work is factory prepared. A man alone can see to the rest." He was gratified by my obvious wonder, as indeed were the other two now. He commented in Finnish, they laughed together (Pekka not seeing that he had conceded something), and again Koivaara translated that they and every Finn considered it perfectly routine to build his own house. Why, doctors could do it, accountants, anyone; he himself was thinking about it.

And the Company helped with such generous loans.

"Yes," he prattled on, "you asked about the Communists. Now that corner house, and the car outside it, belongs to the secretary of our Communist Sports League. In such a big company there are many sports leagues, and one of them is run by the Communists. Do we mind? But please look at that house! He is proud of his house. He is a houseowner. He is also a champion ski jumper. I think you begin to see my answer." Pleased that he had not given too much away, he dismissed the topic and pointed ahead.

"Now please. This is the best." He cleared his throat and steadied his manner, and the chauffeur, understanding, slowed the car. We were close by the water, on a neck of land that ran from a rather swampy beach up a long, widening and tree-scattered rise. A few houses had already been built with the beginnings of gardens staked out. The view was terrific, ample and private for anyone allowed to live here. One could see Tampere over in the distance, by car or bus a mere twenty minutes' run; and all around was deepest countryside. This was certainly the choicest spot. "Yes," said Koivaara, "it is Company land, but land we are selling, almost giving to those who are chosen for houses here. There is much competition. I think you can imagine. So how to decide? Our Managing Director decided it should be for long service, or some other equivalent quality. Only the most faithful servants are chosen. It is a privilege. Perhaps, too great a privilege."

It was becoming evident as to what he was referring. Pekka was looking terribly stony, annoyed, yet flushed with some counteremotion. As we got out of the car to tramp about, he sheered away and stood looking at the lake, at a hole, it seemed to be, made by a fisherman. He had his back to us. We walked up the rise.

"Would you like to see inside a house?" asked Koivaara.

We went inside one; it was a modern interior, finished in different grains of wood, with wide windows and a ranch-style fireplace.

"The owner is only a works manager," came the PRO's whisper; "like our friend Suusanen, he is self-educated. It is a chance for such men. Wouldn't you think it was a chance?" He sounded both wistful and puzzled. He looked out of the window at Suusanen, whom he couldn't understand, and whom he didn't like, but whom, because he had been given the order, he had to win for this Company scheme. The Company had to feel it was beneficent, with regard to every single employee. In fact, as he had claimed, this was its main aim—at this stage of wealth and tradition.

"I hope our friend will think carefully, when the offer is formally made to him. So far, I have broached it only."

We thanked the housewife and returned to the car. Koivaara said something to Pekka, in a half-sporty chiding tone, then quickly went on talking to the chauffeur. Pekka didn't answer. We drove back at speed.

Yet Koivaara seemed pleased by the trip. Just sight of the place must help his task and woo this singularly obstinate man. He turned from the subject and elaborated on other ways in which the Company strived for the welfare of those in its charge. The Bishop himself had blessed its activities. A Christian could feel at ease as its servant.

"But I imagine this aids profitability?"

"Of course. We are in business. It is a very moral union." He looked very certain about this point.

"And this afternoon you are the football referee?"

"Yes. One factory is playing another. Mr. Suusanen, I think, will bring you to the match. He has always been a fan; he used to play goal."

A few minutes later we were back at the factory, still low and gleaming beside the lake. We regarded it in silence, each with his thoughts. Pekka got out and stood very squarely, nodded to the driver and to the man from the office, then motioned me to go along with him. We went back inside. It was a different feeling.

To anyone who has not yet visited Finland, Pekka's attitude earlier in the day, his inability to give any sign that he was glad to see me and show me about, may (Koivaara apart for the moment) seem a bit far-fetched. No. I knew he was friendly underneath. I know that when southerners comment on Yorkshire, on its near-barbaric chill and dourness, they miss the underlying heart (and that when fellow Yorkshiremen scoff at this heart, they do so out of puritan nervousness, or as a joke simply

meant for the family). I admit, Pekka's seeming con-
demnation, at moments, pulled me up, till I got a bearing, so to speak, on Bradford and adjusted for being
further north. His warm heart existed too. Through
screens of caution, through the quick return of a look
that disapproved or snubbed, through the positively grueling silence at times, one hung on—and there, it was
worth it; a ray broke through, not so much a smile as a
nod that signified deep approbation. I had grown up with
this kind of treatment; and though I had avoided it for
twenty-five years, its reappearance was not too daunting.
With patience, one could even love it best . . . so long
as one respected the other person.

As yet I didn't know Pekka well, but I certainly respected him. We shared enough of the same inbred values
—what I had sensed that night of the war—to provide a
basis for understanding. The rest would follow. Never
mind the style.

Even, through this, I liked Tampere more widely.
The slow seductiveness of the north!

Anyway, after the tour was over and Koivaara gone,
Pekka relaxed. Back in his office he fumbled with his
papers, gave them a smack and threw them in a tray.
"Come," he said, "we look again. One more time. Is
that right?" "Absolutely right." I felt like jollying him.
His stocky figure, with its limping stride, no longer
sought a masonic pace but that of the fighter he essentially
was. He certainly regarded this factory as his. To the
Company, to those distant directors who also dealt in
banking and insurance, he might figure just as one of

their men, as one they had agreed to gamble on. One could be sure he didn't return their thoughts. Within his orbit he was commander, all his energies given to the task, the exacting daily production schedule. This was now his fighting outlet, whatever the past issues had been. He was not a man to cease from struggle.

"Football match. Is it good? You are hungry?" For the last time we were passing the frames, the half-filled spools cut by the hooter; one could still hear the high-pitched whirr, and the click next door of the stocking machines, and the clatter of looms, though all were silent. We still spoke as though the noise were deafening in that way of studying each other's face (and which now helped me to realize in him a score of factors I couldn't yet account for); and then outside in the yard there was a hush, and we rediscovered our normal voices.

We couldn't of course converse very much. I could speak to him in Swedish, but he hated people doing so. He would freeze at the first Swedish phrase. I additionally had a dozen phrases in Finnish, so that left us with pigeon English. He was becoming keener on using this, his shyness producing each word like a joke. "Hungry, yes? No food . . . today!" This said, he stumped off to the bus stop. It looked as though our fast must continue.

However, at the Company sports field, which was nearer to an older plant in town, there was a stall with coffee and frankfurters and doughnuts, and he permitted me to treat him here. He ate rapidly, thrusting down the food, then gave me a friendly slap on the shoulder. "Good. Thank you. You, mmm . . . football?"

"I used to play." I mimed childhood.

"Yes?" He followed my inadequate gestures with a deep and serious concentration.

"Outside-left. I liked running." I mimed running, then sketched the field.

"Good." His brows knit more deeply, his whole face given to the problem. Something profound about it puzzled. He stood patiently as though before a wall that had quite impossibly risen before him. What could it be? Around us a group, presumably of other Company employees, though from none of them could you have guessed that an event of any excitement was about to begin, or that they spent their working lives together, were concentrating on this problem too. Coated and hatted, with uniform intentness, they were staring at the space left by my hands. I felt I had better mime it all again. "You understand?" I queried of Pekka, beginning to share the intrusion of worry.

"Oh yes!" He laughed. They were all laughing. They were suddenly revealing the end of a joke. He slapped my shoulder. I was a Simple Simon.

My first taste of Häme humor.

The players were coming out, with Koivaara athletic as the referee. A fast game followed. Volutes of speed. Slides, leaps, as though against a current, as though on skates or jumping skis. The snowbound winter was still in their limbs, and they passed and shot with a pretty good sense of how the ground divided up and to which square the ball should go. Koivaara was as fast as any of them. It was good-class football; it was additionally a paean to the hard emerging vigor of spring.

Pekka and the others occasionally roared. At moments

they groaned with disillusion. Mostly they stared with loaded silence, and with steadfastness as the sun disappeared and the cold of the afternoon set in.

Afterwards, he was more friendly than ever, wagging his head and soliloquizing as he let his hand rest on my shoulder; then without, it seemed, prior meditation he teamed up with three fellows standing near, whom previously he had not acknowledged. Measured talk in Finnish followed. We set off together. Then he nodded to one of them to walk by me; and this one revealed he knew English, from America (though if Suusanen had not beckoned to him, would he ever have chanced a word?), and he told me that they were going to the sauna, to the Company sauna in the next street. "There will be a crowd. Have you tried one yet?"

"Oh sure"—to foreigners with an American background, one always tends to ape the idiom—"Sure. Several times."

"That's great. The sauna is a great institution. But people in America, for instance, that I knew didn't care to expose themselves. They got it wrong."

"Sure. It does you good."

"That's right. That's why we Finns use the sauna." He seemed assured that I was a regular guy, and fell into an amiable silence. He had a hard-bitten bespectacled face. His movements were quiet and conciliatory.

This particular sauna, just one of the half million (for a population of four and a half million) built in every corner of the country, was on a scale that befitted the paternalistic founder of the firm—that is to say, Lars's grandfather, who, with Bible in his buttoned-up frock-coat, might have been quite willing to see the then Russian masters of the country deal suitably with troublesome workers, but who equally for the meek, the obedient, the disciplined, had set up a range of amenities with the zeal of some pioneering Quaker. This sauna could be called his monument (as incongruous stylistically now as a London railway station, but vast), a place in which to be cleansed through and through and issue forth a man of God. It had been renovated following an air raid during the last war; no one had dared dismantle it. Partly of timber, partly of concrete, it hummed from within like a Buddhist temple. The name of the founder, Henrik Stromfors, was still inscribed over its portal.

We had to wait our turn. In an outer chamber, rigged up now as a cafeteria, we drank a slow premeditative tea, sinking naturally into silence. This was not the mean, barbed silence, nor the anxious, overwhelmed-by-life silence, nor any of the other impenetrable silences drifting among Finns like fog, but an inclusive, a friendly, a reverent silence gathering us properly into the occasion. It was my fifth sauna since arriving in Finland, and I had noted variations in approach, some being more chatty than others—my welcoming sauna had been positively skittish, but in general the ground of the occasion was a sober, prayerful frame of mind. Man came here to be renewed in heart through this exercise of the body.

At last we entered, with an issue each of hand towel and birch whisk. We undressed and padded naked to the washroom beyond which were the sauna chambers. I remember, at school, we were constantly naked, scuffling and slipping under the showers, or racing, dressing as we went, toward the library, where the Quaker day began with prayer, but were we conscious of each other's shapes, of differences, except passingly? In later life when these differences have grown, when stomachs and chests have bulged and sagged, and hairs sprouted to a thick mat or thinned down long weedy legs, and faces are grayer, with cares and defeat, and chins have doubled, and the pubic region lost its pristine innocence, it is less easy to be so unaware. Usually, after all, one only sees one's own body, and the quite different body of the other sex, and one's children's bodies chiefly noted for whether they are toughening up—and maybe also there are moonlight occasions, in warm seas, when you all go bathing. I know, a French acquaintance of mine regards this Finnish sauna as barbaric precisely for this: the trooping together of gross male bodies who wash themselves and loll in the steam and beat themselves, all solemnly together—oh la la! When each could be at home in his apartment bathroom, gazing at his wife's shelf of perfumes, catching the good smell from the kitchen? As obscene, my acquaintance concludes, as Auschwitz.

He may have been unlucky. Finns have good bodies. They bring a natural vigor to the sauna that the more urbanized men of the west could not do. Though they age also—though not so quickly, just because of this one remarkable institution.

So I entered with them already a believer in the therapy we were to undergo.

In the dry chamber the thermometer reading was, roughly, one hundred and eighty degrees Fahrenheit. Not all the men were coming in here, some seemingly pre-

ferring the assault of the steam chamber without preparation. But Pekka's group had headed here, each of
us leaving our whisk in a pail ready for the later stages.
It was dark-wooded, weak electric-lit, a cell with steps to a
ten-foot gallery with two facing wooden slatted benches,
and wooden slats along the floor. I additionally carried
a cool piece of wood, so as not to feel my bottom burned,
and I perched on this like a fakir because it was too
hot to put my feet down. Nobody else found it so. We
sat there bunched together, waiting for the sweat to
come. I blew on my arm—a trick I had observed to test
the tinder-dryness of the air. Okay, as yet no discom-
fort; only the overall power of the cell to suck the moisture out of me into its low timbered hull. The light
glimmered. The gloom fixed one. This was the door into
purgatory, the moment to trust oneself to grace, for as
soon as the sweat began to flow the later processes must
unroll.

But no hurry. Nothing to be hurried. The cult must
not be shorn of a minute.

Sweat. At last, patches of dampness beginning to bub-
ble and trickle together, till suddenly one was afloat in
moisture, slipping in ooze, oozing faster than the thirsty
atmosphere could absorb. Ten men, oozing and glisten-
ing, and soulfully brooding the start of the sauna.

"Come." Pekka seemed always to be leader. We followed and picked up whisk and pail, and took a little
warm water in the pail; and, a group of five, went next
door, into the steam inferno. Again, a gallery with slatted
benches, but in front of this, in front of the steps mount-
ing to it, the brick-covered furnace, and enough space

for three or four men to wet their whisks in the pails they carried, to make sure they were soft and whippy, then flick the whisks into the opening of the stove (each after a decent interval), straight in at the fiery stones, to raise a new hiss of steam.

Madness. Each time I experienced this panic, as my skin jumped and my heart raced and my breathing folded up before the attack of wet choking air. The temperature appeared to double itself, and once on the platform, my pail between my feet, my first need was to hang my head, dumbly, like the dumbest of beasts, to pause and discover if I was going to endure. One waited for the next blast of steam with lungs seized up and suspended. Fish, eggs, vegetables, meat: any of these would be nicely cooked. How did man so cleverly survive?

Then, somehow, it was not so bad. Like the others I dipped my whisk in the pail and, starting at the extremities of arms and feet, gently and sedately whipped myself. A nice sensation, and not out of place in this sacrificial chamber. Bring that evil blood to the surface! Sweat, ooze, gasp, smart, till the inner man shall win release from the aches and sloth of yesterday. More steam! Wilt! Be wrung through and through so that a right mind be forthcoming.

One soon got into the swing of the thing——

Alas! Thought too soon; some fellow penitent, or fellow priest, doused the furnace, so that an immense cloud of steam hissed forth as though to give us a flash of the Devil, and I for one was quickly descending, off that platform to ground-floor level.

I swear that the others were about to groan, but they somehow turned it into a laugh.

Another point regarding the sauna—the good humor it certainly gives rise to begins within the steam chamber.

Time anyway now for a wash, for a good rubdown with soap and brush. This was rather better done, in my experience, in the Turkish baths of the Middle East, where the practitioners in those more Sybaritic temples knead the last dirt from one's pores. But no point in caviling; there was also here an ancient toothy buxom matron, busy at the moment among the footballers, making sure they were soaped and soused and massaged free of any lingering pains. Left to oneself, there were hot and cold taps, before which one sat on a low stool, soaping the hollow of one's back with one's whisk; then showers, a deliriously heady experience as one alternated extremes of temperature.

Then back into the steam once more.

At this point the country Finn would be preparing for the final challenge: to plunge straight from the hissing inferno into snow or icy lake (a practice he has followed for at least three centuries . . . he assures the visitor . . . without coming to harm); and I remembered that in 1940, while we were stationed at Joensuu ferrying the refugees westward, we did try out that caper. We were invited to the sauna of a nearby farm, where the birch were already black and silver and the ice was puddled and the thrush were flitting against a pale almond sky. We had been helping this farmer, in between shifts of ferrying the refugees, for the sheer pleasure of felling trees and feeling the good earth again, as the spring broke, with a rush of flooding water, over this northern country; so that suddenly he had said, through our interpreter . . . "Tomorrow I will heat the sauna for you." So, game for the experience, we had sweated and gasped in the smoky interior of a farmhouse sauna, then we had run for the snow! And rolled in it. The most extraordinary sight. And the most delicious experience! If memory ran true, one of life's best thrills. Which was why, returning to Finland now, I needed no preliminary conversion.

Sauna mad. It may seem banal for yet one more person to comment on the sauna, yet how to comment on the Finns if one doesn't?

On this occasion it had worked wonders with Pekka. After the final sluicing down, and a leisurely drying of oneself, and dressing, so that we each had a pink baby face staring out from our crusty clothes, he had lost his usual deployment of reserve and prejudice and broody involvement to become drily talkative and smiling. I was now fully introduced to his friends. They were gesturing the need for a drink. They were becoming unself-consciously hearty. Pekka was emphasizing a suggestion, with a beefy laugh, and now even in Swedish he told me it was agreed that we should dine together. On one side I was to have "the American," on the other a big doughy-faced man who spoke Swedish. "I do not speak Swedish," said Pekka in Swedish, "but my friend is our Union organizer. He requires it. He can explain to you many things." He waved aside having said so much in a language he did not profess to use. A moment of making things easy for people. He smiled sagely, patted my shoulder—as though I were a "likely lad" (Yorkshire idiom)—and threw a patriarchal glance about the group. We had collected three more chaps in the sauna.

Eight all told.

Eight for dinner.

Seven men. Who were they exactly? They were employees of the Company . . . from the four local factories . . . who had risen from the floor to posts of authority, as the American told me, through long service (and tough character—he didn't have to say this), and through the confidence of their Works Committees. Between them they had various night school diplomas, but only he had won a degree. He was an American-trained engineer.

Essentially, they were seasoned comrades. And—out in the street one remarked it, as the chill air caught us again—they could have been a posse of bailiffs, with the same interchangeable flinty jaw and square forehead and watchful eye. But the estate they watched was increasingly their own. They lived in a managerial epoch.

Pekka, if at all, differed only in that despite his calm air of leadership he held on to reservations. Having launched us on the festive evening, he next had to hold back a little. There was a momentary truculence, a critical pause—with that deepening of the gray in his eye that accompanied doubts about himself. Then the sauna mood surged up. He led on. And, once inside, it was he who ordered the first bottle of akvavit.

He had chosen a restaurant (a *ravintola*) that was part

of the building that also housed the Workers Theater
and its cellar offshoot, and on the third floor the Lenin
Museum, but for all that the doormen and the waiters,
as also those who had last done the decor, understood
the rise in status of their so-called worker clientele, and
a lush bourgeois scene confronted us. We might have
been accountants, or managing directors. We were shown
to one of the sparkling tables, and waitresses, very mas-
culine-attired in white shirt and bow tie, attended us with
suave discretion. An orchestra played. Couples were dancing, with movements and steps that belonged to the thirties, the men's brawny arms hugging and pulling the
big-bosomed bodies of their partners. A crooner crooned.
Cutlery rattled. The hum was sedate and anecdotal. Over
all, fizzing up here and there, was the early evening glow
of alcoholic commitment.

For no Finn bothers with a passing glass to assuage a
passing thirst. Either he does not drink, and suffers, be
it for a week or a month or a year, or he instantly starts
counting in bottles.

Then he drinks very quickly indeed.

At the third bottle of akvavit, swilled down with lash-
ings of beer, our conversation found its head. Perhaps
after the second it was searching and prodding for ways
through habitual reticence, and there were guilty jokes
with regard to milk, and uncertain grins, and a string
of jokes about how Häme people never spoke, and broader
grins; and then the war came into it. They had all
gone fighting. My neighbor on the left was the pudding-
faced man, really steamed from the sauna, and he had
the most unhappy voice, deep and sad as though sound-

ing down a tunnel; and before the drink arrived he
licked his lips, and before the herrings he clicked his
tongue; and, speaking, he looked as though he was just
about to give up the ghost, but what he said was kindly
and thoughtful and not defeated in any way. He remembered the war, but at first he seemed to think that I
had been there in the second part of it (called by Finns
the Continuation War, because continuing from the Winter War, it gave them, at first, a looked-for revenge), and
he referred to the Germans being scared of the woods
and, like the Russians, sticking to the roads, and about
how they had snapped up the Finnish girls.

"Like the Americans over in Britain."

"Yes, war's the same"—he was speaking in Swedish,
"but it was not in the end a popular war. *Det var oss
till ingen nytta*. It did us no good."

"We made our point. The Russians respect us. All the
world, I think, respects us." The American had joined
in, in Swedish, his spectacled eyes glinting pedagogically.

"Oh yes. That's true. What you say is true. But it
was in the end heroic suicide. And then, the discipline
turned slack. A number of officers were shot, in the
back. It was a bosses' war. It was not the same as the
Winter War. Look how we have paid for it since."

"You don't think we ought to have fought it?"

"Oh yes, we had to fight. I don't mind fighting. I had
some good years in the woods. I afterwards married a
girl from Karelia."

The American was silent. The first few drinks had already taken him further than the rest of us, and he was
struggling still against this current, his voice indetermi-

nately spiky. While Mr. Puhtimaa, sighing on my left, was equably and thankfully absorbing the liquor. But they were both conciliatory at a deeper level, and a minute later they were agreeing that Mannerheim, though no doubt a brilliant general, had been no friend of the working classes. "He did what he did to protect his own kind, and so as to secure this country as a base in his lifelong struggle against the Bolsheviks. That was how he saw it. What do you expect? He would have been willing to bring back the Tsars."

"I agree. I distrust our Communist neighbors, but it was they who acknowledged our independence, first in 1918, then 1920."

"And they didn't rescind it after this war."

"No, we are the only people on their frontiers who in Europe tonight drink as free men."

They hesitated. Did it call for a toast? Then the American solved it, and stood up, and waited for the attention of his comrades. "To our country, to Finland!" he proclaimed in Finnish, then said it again for me in English. I took it up in Finnish—*"Suomen malja!"* They were delighted. *"Ystävillemme englantilaisille!"* To England, our friend! These toasts went echoing round other tables, and the waitresses, adjudging favorably, brought us little Finnish and British flags to stand among our dishes of food.

"None the less," the American was pursuing his thoughts, speaking to me directly in English, "whereas in 1918 our main internal enemy was the bourgeois, today he is the Communist. We are all Social Democratic men. Men of the Left. We stand for the worker. Yet today we would vote for a Conservative deputy before we would vote for a Communist deputy. The Communist Party remains a conspiracy. Maybe, in wage disputes we work with them. Tactically, we combine—as do they! No one is fooled. Except, I regret, many Finns who ought to know better."

"Yes, could you explain to me why so many Finns do vote Communist?"

"I can. You bet I can." He smiled, the alcohol and perhaps years of explaining this point to Anglo-Saxons giving him an easier manner. "I can do just that for you, sir. Well, do you know our history? Of modern times?"

"You mean, starting with the Civil War?"

"That's right; that's far enough back to go. For then we were defeated by the bougeoisie. Mannerheim and the Right were victors, in May of 1918. The General rode on his white horse . . . while eighty thousand of our men were herded into filthy prison camps. Here in Tampere, how many starved, or died of influenza? How many were executed?" He glanced along at Pekka. "His father was shot. Has he told you about that? He will, or he will take you to his Uncle Matti. Matti Suusanen is still a Communist."

"Has Pekka Suusanen been one too?"

"No. Never. That is what I am explaining. We of the Left were temporarily defeated, and maybe because we had taken to arms, rather than trust to the democratic process. But revolution was in the air! The Bolsheviks had stormed the Winter Palace! Our own Red Guard got out of control and forced the hand of our parliamentarians! So . . . we paid for it. We had to start again, under our leader, Väinö Tanner. But those who would not start again, democratically, but trusted to force, joined the new-formed Communist Party. Maybe, it was because they couldn't forgive the outrages of the Civil War."

"Equally horrible on both sides."

"Oh sure, sure. Plenty of old scores to settle. The peasants were not too fond of the landlords. The workers were not as you see them today."

"Okay. But look, all that occurred fifty years ago. Since then you have fought a war of survival, that drew the whole nation together. So how can it affect the voting now?"

"Like father, like son! The vote is in the family—at least, among the factory workers. The worker himself may now be affluent, and own a car and a washing machine, but if his granddad was shot in the Civil War, and his father has been a Communist, he will vote that ticket too. Well, some are deserting, but not too many. It is a stable, old-established vote. Their Party works to keep it so. No one works like the Communist Party. They have a school near here for agitators; they run sports leagues, youth clubs, a daily paper. They keep their people with their eyes fixed on the questions that they prepare for them. And then—this is their second field of action—they concentrate on the young workers flocking from the country to the town."

"Who, formerly, would have voted Agrarian?"

"Wait!" He didn't explain this "wait." He adjusted his spectacles, and signaled me to drink. Down went the liquor, and the chaser of beer. "Yes, sir. Now, see.

These farmers' children are insecure when they reach the city. It's new, they are new to factory procedure. So the Party workers bring them to their clubs, and give them friendship and a firm lead, make them feel they are part of something strong! And well, they have to take their time, but it is in one direction: towards the Party. They arrange their lodgings in Communist households. They work them with a couple of simple ideas. They'll watch them at their job—and, as often as not, youngsters start in the building trades, and there the whole setup is Communist. It's soon a question of reading the right paper, and sticking to your mates, and joining the Union. From the Union it's only a step to the Party. That's how it's done."

"But what about you Social Democrats? Your Unions? Don't you compete?"

"We compete. We fight them across the board. But until we have solved our own divisions, we are not as strong as we ought to be. You follow me? I am telling you, sir, of the greatest problem that afflicts Finnish politics—that our big parties tend to splinter. The Communists too . . . but they discipline it better."

"So?"

"That's it. That's our major headache. Some of our defaulters keep drifting back, but others go along with the Communists. That weakens us politically, and industrially . . . it's havoc!"

"Giving the Communists greater control?"

"Well, sure. Because, so long as we are divided, they can beaver themselves in. The principal battle is within

the Unions, and we are fighting with our arms pinioned
. . . with SAK, SAJ, which are the two federations, tus-
sling over rival personalities. The line-up is worse than
crazy."

"How is it outside the cities?"

"Well, mostly, I'd say that the smallholder votes for
the Agrarian Party—which now will be called the Center
Party. Except in the north and the east, where the Communists again are leading in the lumber camps. There's
a whole generation out there who are having to come off
the land, who have money one day and uncertainty the
next. They are used to strict, Bible living—and the Word
now comes to them from Moscow! The Devil's Word, but
they are falling for it."

"That is not an uncommon switch."

"Well, I wouldn't know. We don't like it in Finland."

"So your Communist movement is really very strong?"

He did not answer. He looked at his companions, as
though to check an opinion by their faces, by the strength
of resolution there. Then, "We can meet it," he rallied,
"on the one condition . . . that our economy keeps
straight ahead. That is why, in the 1966 election, it is we,
the Democrats, who have to win. We, not the farmers,
carry the solution." He leaned across me to Mr. Puhtimaa, to repeat a part of this view in Swedish.

They agreed. Politically they agreed completely. That
was the Social Democratic viewpoint.

I asked, in Swedish, "Has Mr. Suusanen ever taken
much part in politics?"

They smiled. The American drawled in English, "Well,
thereby hangs a story. Isn't that so?" he asked his col-

league—*"Inte sant? Vilken svår fråga!"* Isn't that a difficult question?

"He could have done," declared Mr. Puhtimaa. "He should have done, was our way of thinking. For in Union matters he was always to the fore. Before 1939, as a shop steward, he got results like nobody else. Pekka Suusanen was known as a fighter, a great fighter, up to the war. And during it, of course . . . in a different way." His voice faded out, soft and solemn; then he added, "But can it also be said that in fighting there are times for truce and compromise?"

"You mean, he wouldn't compromise? But, look, mmm . . ."

"Mmm, it is difficult." Mr. Puhtimaa also appeared to be thinking further round the problem. He regarded Pekka at the end of the table, of all of them the most obviously authoritative, bullheaded, proud of his origins and of being here in the Workers' Restaurant, and yet indisputably today a manager, a responsible servant of their firm. (As were they, of course.) So surely at some point, compromise had entered.

"Mmm," he continued to hesitate, paused, and clicked his tongue. "It is a difficult question." He sighed soulfully.

The American leaped into the breach. "Our colleague," he said, "is a technical man. To that he owes his rightful advancement. But policy is something else."

"You mean, he didn't take the broader view?"

"Exactly." He seized on the vague cliché. "In politics, it is the broader view."

After which the subject lapsed, at that vital point

leaving me none the wiser, and we addressed ourselves to the Hungarian wine ordered to go with wiener schnitzel.

It was becoming, at least for me, a contest to stay facing this alcoholic blizzard. Akvavit, beer, and now wine; and of these the akvavit was the killer. The first few glasses had been raised in concert, and not otherwise, at Pekka's signal; then it had loosened to drinking with your neighbor, or to accepting a toast proffered down the table. The American was a wary and erratic drinker (no good; he was fast sinking under), while Mr. Puhtimaa was a steady but relaxed, a wholly absorbed and appreciative drinker, down whose throat all liquor passed as if at once to get lost in sand. His big soft face lapped it under, with no change in its weight of sorrow, nor in the moderate stir of opinion he advanced upon each subject. At neighboring tables, well, even at ours, a louder-boring note, a boastfulness, was edging into the breeze of conversation, and Pekka was beginning to look defiant even in the midst of laughter; but Mr. Puhtimaa unconcernedly continued, drinking each time his finger touched his glass, and talking in his friendly graveyard voice.

He was seemingly a man who continued to think about earlier topics in a conversation. A good half hour after we had dropped the subject of the Democratic Party, he returned to it, to reiterate roughly what he and the American had agreed before. The repetition, as he made it, gained weight from the drawn-out, singsong intonation of his Swedish. He gave to it the care of a teller of the same old, oft-repeated saga. Then, after a draught of wine, a draining of the glass as though parched for water, he continued . . . "I was saying, this farmers' government has failed to solve the problems of our country! We carry the farmers. It is we in industry who set the pace, and make up for their mistakes. In textiles alone . . . we have accomplished miracles."

He paused on the thought. No doubt he personally had contributed to these particular miracles. "You see," he said, "we demand good wages, but always in a fair relation to prices, and by national agreement, to which we stick. We are strong, but moderate. We are men of conscience. While year after year this farmers' government has pushed up their own spending immoderately. That's why we have this terrible inflation. What today is the value of the Finmark? Democrats have to win the election."

"What about your Conservative Party?" How like an Englishman talking. I was thinking—production, wages, the state, the currency!

"They broaden the discussions, like our Swedish Party, and our Liberals, and other small groups, but they have not the importance of thirty years ago. I believe that is happening in your country also?" As with many a Finn, he casually revealed a close interest in British affairs. Britain, the States, perhaps Germany, and Russia: those were the countries studied by the Finn, in addition to his neighbors of the Nordic bloc. Otherwise, it was the parish pump.

"Yes," he concluded, with a drawn-out sigh, "the only threat to our evolution arises now from the Communists. Otherwise, time is with the Democrats. As Finland becomes more urbanized, so votes pass to our party. But we cannot relax with regard to the Communists."

So there once again was the clear message of Social Democratic feeling.

We drank. Sweet pancakes with berries were rounding off the meal. A liqueur was being shown by the waitress, to check that this was a firm order. It was. It was one of the berry liqueurs, of oriental sweetness. There was coffee. There were good cheap Finnish cigarettes. The bailiff-sharp expressions had gone; they had become a fuzz of easy answers and of growing self-congratulation. As earlier suggested by Koivaara, though then from a different point of view, one was witnessing the best of all possible worlds, or one that would inevitably become so.

Pekka looked troubled.

His glumness had returned.

One could see that his comrades resented this attitude.

It was perhaps what they had meant about his inability to take the broader view.

4

SUNDAYS IN SPRING

NEXT morning Pekka had more than a hangover. He was sunk in a mood of obstinate gloom. Before the end of that dinner party there had been sharp words between him and a colleague and he had momentarily shouted, rasped, with his fist raised above the table. It hadn't struck. He hadn't more than bellowed for a fleeting instant; and in his face there had been nothing personal. It had been a generalized cry of rage. And the American had whispered to me afterwards, "He's right! We shouldn't forget what we've suffered from the bosses" . . . though the accompanying look also said, You see what I mean? No diplomacy. That's how schisms begin.

Suusanen was an unpredictable animal.

In fact, it rather looked as though Pekka, when drunk, went back to his bare-fisted days when he had distinguished himself in fighting the management (and had been noted by them as a man of vigor), all perhaps to revenge his father. His anger certainly made him younger. I was suddenly recapturing him as he had looked on that bitter night of the Winter War—there was the menacing Socialist from Tampere! It had certainly been difficult these last two weeks always to be sure the two men were the same. The years had wrought considerable changes. But at this point he was bridging them.

Afterwards, glowing, with conciliatory nods first to left then to right, he had sunk back to his older manner. He had begun to notice the effect on his colleagues, and to smile with a dry, blurry satisfaction. They had become such establishment figures. He had leaned back and surveyed the room, that was everywhere swaying, among the dancers and the talkers and those groping to the exit for their coats. He had called for the bill. He had hustled us out. Then in the taxi, immensely silent, he had continued humming with the wrongs that smarted; and his breath had been terrible.

Next morning he was miserable. Contrary to custom, he took his coffee alone; and he had left the building before the rest of us, the students too, as it was Sunday, came to the breakfast table. Aarne got up so we could use the living room, put on a track suit, and flexed his muscles. He drank an extra glass of milk; then he took the skis down to the cellar and brought up some of the summer tackle, some long and medium fishing rods, spinners, and various artificial bait. He joined his father for a time in the yard, mooching about in tune to his mood, then came up to eye his mother. She, it could with justice be said, was quietly making the most of the occasion, for after brisk cooking preliminaries, she changed her dress and set off for church. The Bible, as usual after Sunday breakfast, had been placed in the center of the table. The students were noticing it, uncertainly, as though it called to them. Aarne came up and put on a record.

The yard soon after became busier. Pekka returned to the flat for an instant, in silence, looking morosely contrite, not knowing quite what to do with himself even on his own premises, though beneath this burned continuing obstinacy as if the feelings unleashed last night were still valid and must find their target. He looked at the Bible placed on the table, and at the merrily turning disc, disregarded both, and stumped out; and went across the yard and off towards the lake. The sun skipped up from behind a cloud and threw streaks down the path at that instant.

In the yard, all age groups were busy. Well, there were no extremely old people. One rarely encountered very old people—as elsewhere, say, in pubs, or gutters, or cleaning up after great-grandchildren—though they existed, as could be seen from the newspapers where every ten years their birthdays were lauded. Possibly the climate made them look younger. Or, the solution could be that of the Suusanens, who had an aunt, sensibly, in the Old Age Home—a magnificent building beside the lake—and who had this near-mythical Uncle Matti tucked away in the nearby country. One certainly encountered old people in the country.

But they apart, many elders were active on a Sunday morning beating their carpets, on the carpet-beating frames that edged the yard, just this side of the washing lines that all around this city estate, with the grass and the mound and the flag in the center, fluttered with the predominantly white of the washing. Far more of this happened on a Saturday, but the carpet-beating, like sauna-beating, was a widespread compulsive need, and so overflowed into Sunday, despite those who went to church or watched divine service on their screens. Concurrently, rubbish pails were being carried down to the covered refuse trailers that were wheeled away usually on Mondays. There were a good number of cars parked, and these were being hosed and polished; and though it was only the middle of April, some families were setting off to motor to their lakeside huts (which would be the center of their life in summer) to see to the state of disrepair. Into the car boots went axes, gum boots, rope, paint cans, and sometimes bundles of suitable clothing, for apart from the much-favored track suit, some of the grown-ups, especially the men, were still dressed as if their intention, or at least their duty, was to go to church. Dark suits and white collars, trilbies, polished black shoes . . . only the dark spectacles suggested that they were off to a day of leisure.

The teen-agers, those in evidence, those not in cafés or moving in bands from one cinema poster to another, or again those not quietly studying or eking out their student money with a stint of Sunday work in a factory, also in the main favored track suits; and they played *pesäpallo,* a form of baseball, or rode around aimlessly on bicycles. Only Aarne had a motorbike in our particular yard.

The still younger folk played at gangs, American names emblazoned on their jackets. They were ceaselessly active, and roughly noisy; yet the overall impression was of gawkiness and uncertainty about how to combine in a gang. They would suddenly all be sitting oafishly. They had great difficulty in returning a greeting.

But then, people didn't greet each other much.

They were all so engrossed in shouldering their lives.

Wanting to give Mrs. Suusanen a present, I went off to the station for flowers. The wayside kiosks could not be relied on, but the station did a fast Sunday trade, also in fruit and tinned groceries that were not otherwise available. The station was a great local center for loungers, and illegal traffic in alcohol (I was told), which also (I was told) was why the gypsies were much in evidence there. Gypsies in Tampere were frowned upon as lacking in decent civic virtues, but they served miscellaneous ends. They wandered up and down the main street, utterly improbable if caught in a vista that included a factory wall and chimney.

The outer hall of the station was crammed. Beside the shoppers, and coffee-drinkers, and milk-drinkers, sedately standing, and the quest for magazines and postcards, there were groups flocking in with rucksacks, pressing through for cross-country trains, and others with only the look of going somewhere, and a few laden for big destinations such as north to Rovaniemi, or Kemi or Oulu, or south to Helsinki, or west to Turku. Seats arranged as though in a theater occupied one-half the hall, and here among those who had arrived too early sat the occasional weary drunk, inclining his head lower and lower until it hung above the floor. Smart youths walked up and down, and some as though to nab a defaulter before he got beyond their territory. Menace hung beneath the noise of train announcements and freight clatter, and it was intensified by the shut expressions of all those sitting and watching, as of people who would not interfere.

Flowers were extremely expensive; a quite ordinary bunch could cost a pound sterling, so it was accepted that one just gave a bloom or two. Should it be three roses, two carnations, or the slenderest impression of freesia? Whatever it was it would be wrapped and tied into a hooded paper casket, elegantly, as if for jewels; and the unwrapping by the receiver, in this case by Mrs. Suusanen, would be lingeringly and deftly performed, with anticipatory murmurs of pleasure, which when the few stalks were produced (to an English eye, utterly shaming), turned into a crescendo of delight.

Today it was no different. She seemed genuinely touched. She admired each of the three blooms separately; then for each of them she produced a slender vase, and set one on the table and one on the sideboard and one on top of the television set. Three red roses, sighing at one another, but for her they filled the room with spring.

It was the dinner hour and we were quietly assembling. Pekka still wrapped in silence had appeared, and only answering my greeting with a nod, had given me to feel that as I had shared the previous evening, I must also share his sackcloth and ashes. Well, his mood was more than that, more of a travail, of churned-up unresolved emotion, that seemed to be citing me as a witness not just of last night but of years ago (perhaps, for him, the very apex in memory) when he had been the fighter he still knew himself to be—and hadn't he scars and a limp to prove it?—whatever else had caught up with him now. Well, it was something like that . . . I might be imagining it, but his mood betokened more than a hangover. I was, I had learned, the only person he knew now who had actually seen him that night he had got wounded. A night, his wife said, that had changed him profoundly.

One could see that he occasionally broke out like this. The others were accepting it very calmly. The past was not dead, nor the present accepted, not entirely, for Pekka Suusanen.

To Aarne he said nothing, neither to the girls. To his

wife he made some quiet acknowledgment, and sat with lowered head while she pronounced grace. Mrs. Suusanen overflowed with charity, the hymns singing out through her eyes, the curve of her lips remembering the salutation, and her brow the final prayer of intercession. She was all goodness, all understanding, all raised up unto the Lord. Even if her husband had been a great sinner, instead of a worried puritan soul, albeit one who didn't join the congregation, she would have seen him as saved through the Resurrection. The bishop, she had said earlier to the girls, had preached to them of joy and freedom. The girls had goggled with polite excitement.

They had both been smoking like mad that morning.

The meal was soon despatched. It was a Sunday roast, with potatoes and cabbage, all rather peppery, and a side-plate salad of pickled herrings, with berries, and salted mushrooms and cucumbers. There was milk—oh yes, there was pea soup first; and we rounded off the meal with ice cream; and then of course there were coffee and pulla, the home-made, sweetened bread. But nobody talked. We ate in silence. It was in total contrast to the night before. It was a good roast of beef that called for conversation and for wine or beer or a glass of porter, but neither of the two main participants could come that far on to common ground. He disregarded his wife's elation, and ate solidly, thinking his thoughts, while she understood and ministered to him, but did not further obtrude with words. Even, in order not to distract him, she toned down her joy a little.

So, it was quickly despatched, it was bolted down; then the parents went off, with a nod and her smile, for more coffee with their daughter Helmi. Aarne switched on the television. The girls cleared and did the washing up.

Relaxing now, in an easy chair apiece, we watched events from all parts of Finland. The set stood by a corner of the window, behind it a rough-surfaced wall. The window had decorative curtains, that when drawn were three-quarters composed of a light gray cotton with blue stripes and one-quarter of the same with orange stripes, and when open revealed the window plants, the usual ivies and philodendrons, and begonias, and the difficult aphelandra, standing at the back of a low deep shelf, beneath which was the central heating. To the left was the door to the parents' bedroom; then behind Aarne's chair the dining table, a wall of photos and an alpine print; then behind my chair was the sideboard and a bookshelf, and another chair that stood against the wall with the door leading into the hall; and on that wall there were elk guns, and an arrangement of sheathed Lapp knives. Between our chairs stood a low coffee table, the lightest colored, newest piece in the room, and the floor was covered with gray linoleum upon which, in the part before us that had become the television auditorium, lay a square of off-white carpet. Woe betide anyone who introduced a speck of dirt onto that carpet! No one did; Aarne changed into sandals the moment he came in at the door; and Mrs. Suusanen each day brushed it with a fine special brush for the purpose.

With the parents gone we were more relaxed, could momentarily feel the room to be ours, so that Aarne had already offered cigarettes, and was tapping out a rhythm with his fingers. There was plenty of snow still in Lapland,

and in eastern Kemi, and down the fringe of Karelia. A blizzard had just blown through Savo. Helsinki harbor was still frozen up. On the screen we could watch it, province by province, thanks to indefatigable photographers, without having to travel a step. Indeed, it was doubly pleasant because, outside, in Tampere, the sun was shining.

"Your father was rather silent today."

"Oh yes. I believe he has a headache."

"After last night! The akvavit."

"You had a good party?"

"He enjoys drinking."

"Oh yes. Perhaps. Perhaps, sometimes." Aarne extended an easy tolerance. "He has gone now to see my sister. There he will get good strong coffee." He looked about to see if the girls had cleared the coffee kettle away.

"You want another cup?" I rose to serve him, so used to being host at home.

"Don't trouble, please. I think it must be finished." He also rose. "Is there still enough?" He refilled our cups, and passed the pulla. "You would like to hear my new record?" He smiled invitingly. The true end of talk. He politely went to tell the girls about it too.

We all sat intent before his purchase.

An hour later he shot off on his bike, so moved by the jazz it could have been a trapeze that took him soaring from the yard, while the girls and I went for a walk. Already the sun was thinning out. We wore thick coats, and through the streets of the town the chill wind clung to our faces, but along Pyhäjärvi, the southern lake, its wooded slopes protected from the north, the comparative warmth slowed us to a saunter. This part was called Pyynikki, with a panoramic tower and a swimming beach, and an outdoor theater where the auditorium, shaped like a vast sun reflector, revolved to first one set then another, to a war-ravaged trench, or a farm, or a sauna, constructed around it beside the lake. The star piece here was *The Unknown Soldier,* adapted from the novel of Väino Linna.

"He is listened to by everyone in Finland. He has told us so much about our country." Here they blushed slightly. Two days earlier, returning from coffee and cakes with Linna, I had told them of his earthy countryman's idiom, as given to me by a deadpan interpreter. They had blushed then. They were blushing for it still. The taller girl added, "He is full of surprises."

"You mean, he writes about the Civil War, that no one thought it was decent to mention?"

"I think he is very frank, yes. He is fair, we feel." She looked at her roommate. "He is very idealistic for Finland." For no apparent reason they laughed. The blushes died out of their cheeks.

We continued by the lake. The water was placid, colored with pink as the sun died away. The first weekend boats with outboard motor were running back toward the harbor, throwing ripples between the rocks. We stood watching. It was the end of winter, the lull, so short it could hardly be called spring, before the uprush of summer.

We talked about other people in the town. About Matson, the translator, about Kaivanto the painter, about Eeva-Liisa Manner, whose play, *Uuden Vuoden Yö,* was playing to packed cellar audiences. It was a play like a scream of terror in the night. I hadn't been able to follow a word of it, but it had held me (its first two acts) as though I too were a Finn confronted with its blast at my Finnish inability ever to get out of my shell, despite its realistic orgy of drunkenness and sexual provocation and insult (especially at a pastor), leading to inevitable suicide. Very much under the skin. The girls, who felt they should meet everyone, see everything, in view of their career, ran out of words when we got to it in English, but chattered wildly to each other in Finnish. *"Vaikuttava ja aito"* was a phrase I understood—strong and true. These thoughts elated them.

They curbed themselves. "And, please tell us, what do you think of our professors?" They had seen me once or twice at their college.

"Of course, very nice. But a bit managerial? Americanized? You know, as if it were the hierarchy of some cartel? I am always getting this impression in Finland; and that the next step, for the more ambitious professors, is into some top political caucus. One doesn't feel that in the secondary schools, or technical schools, or in adult education."

"You think that the teachers are better there?"

"Not better. More simply defined as teachers."

"You have seen many schools?"

"Quite a number now, here and in Helsinki, and during those three days I was in Turku. The main town schools. But say if I'm wrong. Of course, all the young crave for education, and you'll study on a pittance and pile up debts so long as you can pull through to a degree. But, aren't the textbooks a bit old-fashioned, and the teaching methods a bit too wooden, and isn't the professor's word too godlike—when he isn't writing Party manifestos?"

"It could be. Yes. This is often debated." They further debated it between themselves, somehow carried beyond surprise, surprise not unmixed with outrage, that otherwise as Finns they would feel at a foreigner voicing criticism. But they were used to me now. They had got beyond those first dossier-filling days.

"It is so important for us," the taller one said, the girl who came from Haapamäki, "to matriculate out of the Gymnasium. It would be terrible to leave from the Middle School, unless, of course, to become a secretary. We study, we do not think beyond our subject. There is always no time—like no accommodation!" She laughed slyly. She was becoming more sporty, working up towards her Chelsea summer.

"But we have to succeed!" her colleague prompted her, vaguely disapproving, perhaps more aware of the sober Sunday walkers, with their children, passing on the main path above us. "Later we can debate these questions."

So we too soberly moved on.

But education was an emotive subject, as emotive as *Uuden Vuoden Yö*, because for the young who did not matriculate, who did not win their white cap, a lower social status followed (as certainly as it would do in England); and though these two were over the barrier, eligible for the right dances and boys, it remained, as their parents must have made it for them, an issue that easily worked them up. It was becoming quite an afternoon. They were open almost to any topic after such preliminaries.

"It was still winter, and mostly night.
Dusk filled the afternoons."
Heikki Havas

*"Tampere a quarter of a century later . . .
prosperous and confident."*

*"They had been told
by their mothers—
'behave
as if in church!'"*

*"We were linked
in the Lutheran underworld."*

"*Nor any of the other impenetrable silences
drifting among Finns like fog.*"
Nyman

*"This is the Company's proudest achievement.
A man likes to own his house."*

"They are used to strict, Bible living—
and the Word now comes to them from Moscow."

*"Walpurgis Night
and the first of May,
called here Vappu."*

*"Seeking extra privacy in
this very private neighborhood."*

So that when, pursuing my interest in Pekka, I laid an innocent snare in that direction, they went for it as usually they would not do.

"Yes," they agreed, "that is the big discussion! It is almost a quarrel—no, never quite a quarrel. You say he took you to see the land yesterday? Oh yes, so he must be about to accept it! He wants to, we are sure; he longs for the country, to hear the first lark in spring—we are all like that. The Finns are countrymen. But, even more important, it should be a gift for his wife, to thank her for her sacrifices. For it was her strip of forest from her father that was sold for Olavi's and Marjatta's education. Schooling has to be paid for, as you know, after the elementary stage—at least, some expenses. It is not here free. They have had debts for years, though now they are clear. And last year was her fiftieth birthday—you have seen the photo by the dining table. The top one. So . . ."

Such a rush of words! Both girls seemed abruptly to have been struck dumb when, catching their breath, eyes sparkling, they paused and didn't know who should continue. The shorter, more circumspect one, began, "That is how it is," as though to close the subject. How swiftly came these complete reversals!

I prompted, "But I don't think he is accepting . . . at least, not without the most grueling degree of self-catechism. He is unable simply to take such a gift, from the Company, the bosses—the Whites, if you like. . . ."

"But he is now a manager! He has accepted that. After all these years, he has earned the very best. Like his higher salary, it is only a reward." The taller girl challenged with argument, adding, "Mrs. Suusanen says this to him. Aarne says it to him. So does Helmi. We have heard the discussion. He has no good answers."

"To my ear," I said, admitting that I listened, "Mrs. Suusanen always defers to him. She understands that he cannot suddenly become too much of a Company man. To be a technical boss in the factory is one thing; to have a privileged house by the lake is another. He is suspicious of becoming a Welfare exhibit. Here, in a municipal flat, he stays free."

"I think so too," the shorter one said. "It is hard for him. We have also debated, in view of his past, what he should do. He cannot totally renounce what he has fought for."

"Yet you believe that finally he will accept?"

"Yes, finally. He will reconcile his views."

"After he has tormented himself to the full?"

"Oh." They were embarrassed. "He will decide rationally. Finally, he will accept it for his wife."

"I suppose there must be other factors." But for them the topic had run its course.

But what a lot had been said! What a spring-cleaning! Shakily they were beginning to realize this. They muttered something about "must be going back." We retraced our steps, eyes on the path, on the lake, on the blue band of sunset. At the first street we muffled up again for the brisker walk across town.

Though then it was that the shorter one thought to say, "It is a real problem for a man like Mr. Suusanen. He is a very good type of Finn."

"I feel it. He is a man of principle. And one coping with a fast-changing world."

"I think in him you are able to see a big part of our recent history."

Eyes pointing chastely ahead, they sped us back to the warmth of the flat. In their room they were whispering for hours afterwards. Giggles. Coffee steaming. Then, their typewriters.

That was two weeks ago; while last weekend I didn't see the family till Sunday, as I had been in Helsinki celebrating, among crowds of aggressively white-capped students, Walpurgis Night and the first of May, called here *Vappu*. Like the Japanese in flower-viewing time, who change from being well-regulated citizenry into revelers of every sort, the Finns, at this official start to spring, let go in public. Parties ring out of every street, with toasts and heroic songs till dawn, and break-aways to other parties, and to roaming the town in exultant bands (that at midnight are ranged around Havis Amanda, the watery statue down the Esplanade), and girls as much as boys go crazy; and though this year there was a freezing wind, the keg upon keg of liquor opened poured heat over the city, and so of course there were terrifying drunkards, collapsed about the streets like meteorites, or swaying, it could be to ancient hymns, ancient shamanistic dirges, unseeing from one corner to the next; and as day came up there were Communist parades, watched skeptically by the bourgeoisie, then more feasting in family settings.

Not a start to May one was likely to forget, though the following morning, Sunday, in the train, things had shaken back to normal. Discreet voices, hushed faces, sober, neat attire and posture. The comfortable seats all facing one way, with a central aisle down which it would have been appropriate for a sidesman to pass the plate. I couldn't but recall another journey, from Salonika to Athens by train, the carriage so convulsed by talk, and crackle of papers, and throw of dice, that people, those Greeks, kept moving around as in musical chairs for any spare seat, to make certain that no stranger was left who hadn't heard their views about the world and who hadn't replied with his own credentials. Or a Spanish train, any number of trains, with pedlars and singers and well-bred discourse. Or the trains in India with their sham swamis and forums of metaphysical argument. But here, even more than in England, reticence clutched at voice and gesture, to a model, presumably, that could not be faulted.

The Suusanens had finished their Sunday dinner, and I was gently chided for confusing the train times. Olavi and his wife had been there, had just left, southbound for Helsinki—but then, they'd be spending the summer near Tampere. Helmi and her husband, Toivo, were present. Aarne. The girls. There was a postcard from Marjatta. My critical thoughts concerning Finns evaporated before the demonstration of friendship. They asked me how it had been in Helsinki. They forced me to feel I had a toe in their circle. Mrs. Suusanen bustled to the kitchen and brought a plate of food and, as a favor, some beer. This was the other side to churchiness: unobtrusive loving-kindness. I felt so happy to be with them again.

Afterwards, I went fishing with Aarne. The parents, chauffeured by Toivo, and openly urged on by Helmi, who was a woman for whom possessions counted, had gone once again to inspect the land offered to them by the Company. Seemingly, a decision had to be reached. The girls were excited. Aarne was shrugging, today a shade against the idea because of something his brother had said. He referred twice critically to Olavi.

Otherwise, he was in a madcap humor, and we set off on his motorbike as though for the pleasure of scattering gravel and throwing up dirt from the road. The tackle was firmly clamped beneath us. It was a bit late in the day for a fishing excursion, but the intention was more to rip into the country, and to halt by a less frequented lake, and to try a few casts, and to chat and come home. Or, there was an inn out there, he said, with a sauna. Would I prefer to go to the sauna? Not for me, thanks, definitely no. I meant this, but Aarne found it hard to believe me. Olympic fit and keen on challenge, looking for what he could measure up to, he seemed to think that a sauna then a swim (now that the ice had come off the lakes) would round off the outing.

I told him I should hate to miss a moment's fishing. A risky statement, as I knew little about it. I could follow that he wished to practice with a fly, a feathery hackled piece of bait that looked devilish beside some old-fashioned worm, and that for me he had brought a medium spinner, but I had little guidance as to what happened next. I was content for the moment to feel the crisp air, that made every nuance of color sparkle, and to glow with the good dinner inside, and to stay on the pillion. Though he was not going fast.

He started off fast. He would take a corner fast, or overtake a motorist fast; then he would slow for conversation. Sitting on the bike charged his thoughts. "You are all right?" he cried. "I think perhaps you wished to go with my father?"

"No, I'm fine. I have seen the land. Don't you think he ought to take it?"

"Oh yes, perhaps. He is with a good Company. All those old quarrels. . . ." He shrugged and hunched himself for a sharp bend. I bent to the same angle as the speed increased; then, slowing again, he shouted evenly, "My friends are found in every party. Center, Communist, SDP. Good friends! We don't talk politics. My father's friends, they are too narrow-minded. They quarrel; they don't give good advice. And, my Great-Uncle Matti—also thinking of the past! But my father is very independent. He takes his time, but he acts with courage."

"Yes, what happened after the war? When I met him in the war, he was a great rebel. Now he is not a rebel, is he?"

"Oh yes, still, he is very independent!" Aarne laughed, shyly but fondly. He tussled with his father but was devoted to him. "All Finns are independent. I think, after the war, that the factory was told to make cloth for Russia. We had to, I think, for eight years. My father worked harder than anyone, to help clear the name of Finland. He became very patriotic, after the war. I think then he forgot his quarrels."

"I see . . . while working on reparations, he and the Company on the same side, in the same situation . . . he saw things afresh. A big leap. And it has stayed like that?"

"Yes, perhaps. I think, now with the land, he is asking himself that question closely. He has to be sure that he has not surrendered. My brother Olavi is saying to him . . . we shall win the election, so—no need to worry! But I say, that is politics." Aarne's face contracted with impatience. It lost its usual mobile pleasantness. He was stamping on the accelerator again. "Not, I think . . . the way to discuss it." He took on one of his father's expressions. We soared through the countryside.

By the lake, sorting out the tackle, fixing the reels to the fiberglass rods, his a good nine feet in length with a light, fast action at the tip, and mine a more manageable six-footer, with a push-button reel and other fine devices, we dawdled into further conversation because Aarne—I think this is right—needed to talk, and could perhaps best talk to a stranger. As with so many uncertain conversations, its purpose for him was to sort himself out. In fact, this was something he was always engaged on: playing jazz, speeding, changing his factory, donning his track suit, rejecting politics. His dad to date was his favorite hero, but new requirements were edging in, and this for him was a tumultuous process.

"You had another postcard from my sister."

"Yes, she is getting on fine in London."

"I would like to travel. Many Finns cannot see beyond their country, but I will go. Perhaps, to India. Have you been to India?"

"Yes, twice." And in contrast to the soft gloom about us, the settling pink and gray light, between the birch, and by the margin of the water, I was suddenly blasted by glare and dust and the mirages that drought engenders (but not this time with any nostalgia); then it had gone. "As an engineer, you would find plenty to do in India. How do you like your new firm?"

"Better. I get two marks an hour, in addition to my

training. It is now decided, they will allow me to attend the Technical College in Tampere. Later, I must go to the Politechnic. I shall take other exams—for my white cap! I was not able to attend the Gymnasium. I have had to work since the Middle School. But now, little by little, I can study." He was pleased, anxious, envious, confident. Slowly his more complicated future would unroll. He couldn't quite picture himself within it.

"Are you happy with that rod? Look, like this, with the line. Set the float so. Go beyond the tree, where also, see, there is a tree underwater . . . who knows, perhaps you will meet a perch!" By now he had realized that I knew nothing of fishing. He was not taking this aspect seriously.

I followed his instructions, going quietly to the spot, and aimed beyond the weedy-looking water to where there was the semblance of a current, and cast smartly barely daring to look, releasing the line in a blur of excitement, and reeled in slack, and watched where the flat was drifting into a snare of grasses. Then I lifted it and jiggled it, remembering that the bait, a wriggling bit of blade, had to move like a fish, though I couldn't for the life of me see how a perch could be so silly as to be deceived.

No perch was. I cast again, loving the movement of the rod and the moment when the line flicked onto the water, but fearing a strike because I had no desire to know that the hook had caught a fish's throat. I liked eating fish but, as with poultry and meat, shunned the essential act of killing. It was simpler to decide that I was not a fisherman, but a country-lover by a patch of water, who happened to have this spinner in his hand, but was principally watching the decline of daylight, and becoming aware of the immense silence, with somewhere a chaffinch and a crested tit starting out on their summer conversations, settling all about us.

So something took. The reel cricked, and with dismay I began playing the victim, paying out and cranking in, to turn the fish until it was exhausted; and Aarne came up, surprised by my cries that were of the "Oh Lord . . . Oh God!" variety, and netted the brute, a very modest perch; and I thought, "Oh well, I had to catch one, I suppose, so as not to shame him." But I didn't cast the line again.

He caught plenty of small fellows, rudd and roach, and then, wading, in his excitement with the spinner, he landed a large battling perch; and on the way home he talked of trout and salmon that he had caught previous summers. Aarne was a dedicated fisherman, and had wandered the cairns and bogs of Lapland in sporting Kalevalas of his own. He was also a dedicated skier, a cross-country runner, a midweek wrestler. He had told me before that as a child his favorite sport had been to plunge into snowstorms, to lose all bearings, then to puzzle a way home by the small signs that he could just interpret. Now this was happening in the world of men. He was plunging in, and he had to go on, however lost he felt, to new doorways. But beneath that amiable pliability he had, like his father, the courage of a lion.

He was very good company. He had promised to teach me to become by summer a rather better fisherman.

Then, today. Another Sunday. The third Sunday of ripening sunshine, so that the chill came quickly off the window and the children were earlier into the yard. Cars leaving for the countryside left before the housekeeper's husband, devout and regular as an old timepiece, set off for church. Mrs. Suusanen, not finding it politic to follow him, clattered pots and cleared and swept, with a soft, martyred motherliness, till she had us all out of the flat. Aarne and his father disappeared to the cellar. The girls went for their daily inspection of the young birch twigs beside the lake, for them the symbol of the Finnish spring. I hied to the railway station, found Friday's *Daily Telegraph* and Thursday's *Times,* with their reassurance of life as usual back in that southern island I came from, and later I looked in on a painter whom I could touch for a Sunday morning drink.

It is not that I am a particularly avid drinker, but one partial to a glass of beer or a glass or two of wine with a meal, and then a lift at the start of the evening—apart from specific drinking occasions; but since I came to Finland I have been goaded almost to a Finn's method of despatching the glass, or usually it's the bottle, put before him, by the difficulty of getting the fancied nip at the place and moment when I fancied it. And with the difficulty has gone such disapproval ranged against one's request for help. "Can I have a beer, please? Oh, not without food? Well, I'll have some ham. Oh, not here at all? I can have milk? Oh, thanks. In the restaurant opposite? Yes, thanks. Yes, I like milk, and sour milk too. No, I have nothing against milk. I'm being quite serious. Some food, I agree, tastes as good with it. . . ."

". . . Oh here you don't serve beer at the bar? Only spirits at the bar, but beer at the tables? Beer is allowed when one starts one's lunch? . . ."

". . . Oh, I see, if I am in such a hurry—for a drink, that is" (I'd been waiting twenty minutes)—"I ought to have gone to a higher grade of restaurant? Oh! . . ."

". . . But there isn't a bar anywhere! I've looked already down a dozen streets. No, I don't want a meal. You see, in this weather I get so cold, I need a shot of cognac. No, I don't want an illicit bottle. I'd settle for a beer if there was a pub in sight. . . ."

". . . Here is my passport, so I can order what I like? It's not recorded in a book, in the case of a foreigner? So I'll have three bottles of Fundador, your number 3985, and a bottle of 4497, and some 6413, yes, two bottles, and how about 2022 for an akvavit? You have no views upon it? No, it's not for a name day. No, I am not buying it for a Finnish citizen. You see, it is such a walk to get here, and the hours are awkward, and it's all so difficult, I'm just buying it, to have, to offer to people, to have an occasional drink by myself. Oh dear!"—for the square-faced matron, an officer of the government at the government store wielding this monopoly, with Finns along the counter whispering their orders then waiting while the details were recorded in their individual books, then popping the liquor into an attaché case or some such dissimulating carrier, felt, she felt that my attitude was wrong. I can't say why, but I suppose I didn't show that I knew it to be devil's milk. The need was proffered but not the guilt.

So I called on the painter hoping for a sherry, and the chance of again looking at his paintings that were slashed as though the vibrant colors had themselves at that point torn the canvas, but of course all his opened bottles were empty. And as I saw him about to open a whisky and remembered what that in particular did to him, as the need to drain it would speed up, I cried out that I was on the wagon, and he checked himself and his wife brought coffee (and his gestures, I noted, as with other Finns, while handling the bottle had been underlined as though this were the momentous side to life) and after some moments we could talk again as usual. I slipped away back to the Suusanens. It was second-best to sip sherry alone—from bottles hidden in my suitcase and wrapped in woollies against a telltale clink—but no one here understood the sipping. Mrs. Suusanen disliked liquor in the home, bar the little she imported. So I secretly drank, as the girls smoked, and as Aarne toned down his record playing, and as Marjatta perhaps had once hidden her love of crime beneath the pillows. We were linked in the Lutheran underworld.

Helmi was there. It was now a brilliant morning and she had walked over to chat with her mother. She was beginning to look pregnant and, a compulsive flirt, she was hyperconsciously hiding away then pirouetting out for attention. Her golden hair was shaped and sprayed, she had new high heels, she was using make-up. She had once gone in for amateur dramatics, and had worked in a store, and been mad on dancing. Toivo, her husband, however, was strict, with an habitually suspicious glint in his eye, and they were always having minor tiffs.

In relation to the family, what stood out was her obsession with things Swedish. She spoke Swedish, and this had helped her to a higher grade in the store where she had worked—like many such firms, owned by Swedish Finns—and she looked Swedish, with paler cheeks and slimmer

legs than most local girls, and she had a Swedish concern
for money and position, and in Toivo she had married an
up-and-coming fellow, a salesman, mostly of Swedish
hosiery, whom she now was urging to work in Sweden,
where salaries were a third higher. She was explaining this
now again to her mother, moving in and out of the kitchen,
in the Swedish they enjoyed speaking together.

Why this insistence on Swedish, so opposite to her
father's feeling on the subject? Possibly, in this austere,
patriotic family, with its clever older son and daughter,
this had seemed her one chance of the light. Perhaps she
had been abetted by her mother, in whom many a desire
was smothered. Alone, they always spoke in Swedish,
though less so when the men were present. They laughed
together. They discussed people, tore the town apart, argued
heatedly. The usual moderation was absent, so that that
seemed suddenly to be a sexual thing, part of the ordained
marital balance. It was not there now, woman to woman.
A more sprightly Mrs. Suusanen emerged.

"Has Father agreed to accept the land? About time. All
this stuffiness!"

"Yes, and no. He is still debating. For his own part he
has nearly accepted, but . . . next Saturday he will con-
sult Uncle Matti."

"That old crackpot! *Han är vriden!* He ought to think
more about you. You ought to retire. You will like it by
the lake."

"Uncle Matti is his father's brother. Grandad was shot.
We cannot forget it."

"It is time we did! Mother, you have prayed for those
that shot him. Isn't that enough? The world has changed.

We're not workers any longer. Only the Communists think about it." Came a tap of heels, slowly cornering, as something was carried into the living room. They came back quicker. Helmi was laughing. "Toivo is such a Turk! Soon I shan't have a girl friend left." She did not sound too displeased. "You know young Liisa, she has had an abortion. Everyone seems to have had one now. There's so much happening under the surface. The young people stop at nothing." Wistfulness could be detected.

There was a pause. No more. No maternal tut-tutting.

"Shall I carry this in?"

"Please. Helmi, you should stay in Tampere until the child is born. He should be born in Finland."

"He?"

"Of course. I want to have him with me by the lake. Later, if you have to, go to Sweden."

"Toivo is not too keen, fundamentally."

A more meditative silence now followed.

Some minutes later they were prattling again. Gossip from the factory, gossip from the store that Helmi now only entered as a customer, as Toivo, unfairly, had stopped her from working; gossip from between the lines of the press. Tampere sounded like a hive of seducers, an aspect of it I had not encountered.

They sounded so jolly; it seemed so unnatural to be sitting with a glass of sherry alone—wasn't this possibly the moment to chance an assault on the holy household rules? I rushed out, holding the bottle as though it had arrived by post that instant, crying, "Can you forgive me? Excuse me, please. But will you accept a glass of sherry?"

Total amazement. Slow remembrance of the fact that

somebody else was in the flat. Wave of tension—against the stranger, against interruption, against the threat that the bottle offered to habit. Then smiles. A quick and a slow spark of humor. A clearing of the throat. Glasses were taken, spotlessly shining as always, from the shelves. I filled them, three glasses—which fortunately resulted in the bottle being finished, which was dropped, without a pause, into the trash can—and we drank to friendship, and the start of spring, and, hoping to please her, to Helmi's condition.

"This is two weeks together that we have drunk to spring." Mrs. Suusanen recalled the previous Sunday. Like a man she had already gulped back her sherry, and was rinsing the glass. Putting it away.

But she was not holding the incident against me.

One up on the girls. They just wouldn't believe it.

5

UNCLE MATTI

ALL that week the household brooded over the coming visit to Uncle Matti. There was wry speculation, that grounded in silence; there were bursts of irritation and resentment, as though it were they who had been summoned to the presence, to the "conscience of the family," as Pekka considered him, although it was Pekka who told the stories that usually ended by showing that his uncle had been misguided in this course or that. Mrs. Suusanen held aloof. Aarne told me that she would not be going. It was not possible to tease out why, but at another moment it did come out that there was doubt as to whether Uncle Matti and the Norwegian widow with whom he lived had ever been married in church. He had been so much on the move. His life had undergone so many bewildering changes. It was, it came out, so long since they had seen him, for all that he was an ever-present figure in their thinking. The girls added that Mrs. Suusanen much resented Pekka's recognition of this notorious old Communist uncle while he still refused to make it up with his sister, the religious one, who had married a White farmer. Perhaps there were even words about this, for the Suusanens looked more broody together during this week than at any other time.

But Pekka could not resist his memories that rekindled the passion that had inflamed him then (that left him now, once the memory was voiced, looking a bit edgy and perplexed) and, after television, he started up, speaking rather harshly, or somberly, or sometimes it sounded almost a joke. Then he'd turn to Aarne—"You tell that . . . in English." And Aarne would begin . . . "1931 was the worst year for the Democrats. The Lapua Movement nearly seized the government. Yes, and the bosses were profiting by it. They would not take Red employees. I think my father is exaggerating—perhaps all workers were Red then! But, he says to tell you that he was twenty-one, and it was then that he was taken on by Stromfors, and that it was due to Uncle Matti. For he . . ."

But Aarne's easy pace of recounting, and hesitation over certain words, did not satisfy his father, who switched abruptly to the taller girl, demanding that she finish the translation. Which then made clear that Uncle Matti, a part of the outlawed Communist Party (outlawed just the previous year through the pressure of the farmers' Lapua Movement), had instructed Pekka in the Communist technique of pretending to be much milder than one was, in order to attain one's ends later. Pekka had entered the Stromfors factories in a completely "revolutionary" frame of mind, although nominally a Social Democrat and seemingly a rather passive one. He had hidden the rage that burned in him, that had burned steadily since his father's execution (on the same day as his eighth birthday), and that already had lost him three jobs. He had hidden it on Uncle Matti's instructions.

But then, after a year or so, he couldn't stay quiet any longer. He had begun not so much to agitate as methodically to organize his mates. He had found his own voice, a practical one, and not when it came to the point so revolutionary. He burned with feelings against the bosses, but this usually seemed to come out through measures that were also to the Company's advantage.

"But, excuse me," I interrupted, "please say to Mr.

Suusanen that the other evening at dinner his colleagues were remembering that by 1939 he had become the factory's most militant shop steward. That is, he had found the knack of sustaining the workers' views against the bosses." I was also remembering what Lars had said, in that nighttime tent out in Karelia, that in 1940 the Stromfors family had looked on Pekka Suusanen as their enemy, and were more or less hoping he would be killed at the front.

"Yes, yes," he was agreeing, through our interpreter, "on the surface, yes. I won the concessions! The bosses always wanted to dismiss me—but they feared a strike. On the surface we were enemies. But in fact, underneath, to my surprise too, the concessions I won also helped the bosses. Higher productivity followed. Better human relations followed. I had to learn, and I think they had to learn, that in a factory there is a common interest."

There was a pause after this solid conclusion.

"And Uncle Matti?" Aarne prompted.

"Oh yes, Uncle Matti"—through Aarne again now—"my father says that Uncle Matti had to go away to Sweden. He was exiled. His Communism never achieved anything."

So that, if there was one, was the point of the story. . . . Pekka had outgrown Uncle Matti's ideas, and the revolutionary passions of youth, through finding something that worked better. He was a practical man. He was attuned to technology. And then to cap it, his war experience, culminating in the shock of his wounds, had made him more pragmatic still.

Though he had not outgrown, nor could he ever, the

memory of his father's death and the consciousness this imposed on him of some continuing obligation. Hence his seeking out Uncle Matti from time to time, vaguely for guidance.

So, Saturday arrived, and all the women found other things to do. The girls were recovering from a bout of exams; in any case, they weren't invited. Helmi and her mother had booked at the theater for the Tampere production of *The Boy Friend,* which they had already seen twice. Toivo was our chauffeur, Pekka sat beside him, with Aarne and myself lolling in the back; four men, with a good lunch put away, setting off to see Uncle Matti. The three of us, that is, were accompanying Pekka in what at the last moment became something of an ordeal for him. He sat silently over his coffee, long after the time for departure.

Toivo was an accomplished driver and one who looked about for challenge. The Finnish roads were comparatively empty, but there were enough bends, and cars round the bends, to introduce an occasional risk, and Toivo liked thrill and risk. As a driver he sought out the thread extended between life and death. Such escapades have long disappeared, except for madmen, from English roads, but in Finland there is a sporting chance, as you race neck and neck for the bends, that you will somehow clear them, and the oncoming traffic, and even emerge as the front car. Toivo had a Saab, and tuned it daily, so that he could emerge as the front car.

About half an hour out from Tampere we were challenged by a Buick that was just shaking loose from a Mini, like a Pekinese snapping at its heels. We were cruising along, admiring the landscape, the Finns seeming to breathe deeper once they were among the lakes and forests, and I thinking that a certain monotony inseparable from birch and pine, when as here there were no hills or valleys but simply a slow, level unfolding, was well broken up by the blue of the macadam, and the glancing white of the kilometer stones, and the signposts, and then in the clearings by the more detailed domestication. It was landscape that benefited from the hand of man, too repetitious without it. You gazed and gazed at the passing pine, interspersed with the passing birch, and inevitably you were forced deeper into deep Finnish thoughts, while the lakes that naturally lifted you free swept by too briefly when seen from a car.

Most of the tree-felling nowadays took place in the north and northeast of the country, though nowhere on the scale of former years (so that Finland waiting for its forests to be replenished had become an importer of timber to feed its pulp and paper factories), but here and there, as we drove along, sections of forest had been leveled that winter, because some farmer needed the cash, the trees felled and taken by lorry, or pulled along snow tracks by horse sleigh or tractor, to a convenient point on the river-lake system, to be bundled ready for summer floating. There was no one in sight doing anything at the moment, but these bundles of logs, then stacks of concrete slabs and piping, and ditch pumps, and trails of smoke from isolated clearings, testified to human interest, a little mysterious when so completely dwarfed by mile upon mile of gray-green forest, but a welcome variation in the scene.

One's attention however came back to the road, except

when a lake broke into view, for on the road there were other cars, buses and long-distance lorries, and though there was plenty of room for everyone, one never just knew when a crisis or a challenge might demand every ounce of concentration. There was no question, as Toivo changed down and we leaped after the impudent Buick, that had almost swished us into the ditch, of ordinary conversation continuing, or of our paying further heed to the landscape. As though we had been four traffic cops, or four acrobats straining every nerve to yield the maximum co-operation, we bunched about Toivo and measured the problem as somberly and intently as he. Toivo, I should say, was not a somber man so much as a brisk and wide-awake one, conveyed in short sharp glances, for he was not talkative; but in the driving seat he additionally frowned, and gritted his teeth, recognizing that lives and honor lay between the hands of his performance.

We had caught the Buick up but could not overtake it. It filled our side of the road. Toivo promptly crossed the line and had two wheels abreast of the other, when, round a bend, a bus appeared, itself well into the middle. For a fleeting second it looked as though Toivo would head for the opposite verge, so that we and the Buick would pass the bus, if at all, one on either side of it; but just in time he drew back, to our chagrin allowing the Mini to catch up. He was drained of color. *"Hitto! Hitto!"* Then, a gear lower, he was charging again.

Again we had to brake, and this time the Mini tried to pass us on the near side. Toivo quickly had him in the ditch, so that we could see him abruptly coming to a standstill, then continuing but effectively out of the race. We concentrated now entirely on the Buick. As it chose to slow behind a lorry, then swerve out too late to take the lead again at speed, we passed it on a gradual curve, inching it nearer and nearer to the side, so that suddenly the other driver lost his nerve, a fact communicated to each of us, so that we equally entered into Toivo's skill in taking control of the other car, so that it was slowed, slowed, and dismissed behind us. Whining through the gears, we sped ahead.

That was nothing. Now we had to hold the lead against a slightly faster car, driven by a sulking, enraged driver. He kept pounding up against our bumper, which Toivo let him do, braking to help him then slipping free past a cart or a lorry. The road developed a series of switchbacks, on a small scale, around an outcrop; then, through a large village, we were running by a lake, so that at that pace a flick of the wrist would be enough to take one into the water. By now we had been racing for twenty minutes. Toivo signified it was the finish. He slowed, leaving just enough room for the Buick to pass with a wheel off the road, then, as he passed, we braked sharply. The other by now enraged dervish of a driver was so unbelieving of this concession that, as though we had still been neck and neck against him, he continued over on the offside, accelerating, swaying, showing all his skills—but all quite madly with wheels spinning dirt on the inch of ground between verge and water: so that in all it took him a good two minutes before he realized that he could center safely. We had followed at fifty yards, admiring this display.

Seemingly at last the trick became clear to him, for further along, he had stopped and as we passed, he was sitting silently mopping his face.

So, with no further challenge, we finished in the lead.

Not a particularly civilized act, but the Finns relished it. It was a way of checking up on one's nerve, something they all believed in doing. No one would have tolerated a lesser performance. Toivo's face wore its crispest look. He had in fact never had an accident. Besides employing the most meticulous skill, he was too good a psychologist.

Pekka was elated, all thought of Uncle Matti and the burden of the day swept out of mind. Just the mood in which to arrive.

We were now slowing into a village, level with a tongue of lake that broadened to the north with a sprinkling of islets. The rain clouds formed a vast horizon. The gray light was lighter on the water, and very still, and just beyond the village some factory smoke rose vertically. There was an important paper factory here, fed by timber floated down the lake. The works and the housing were hid by trees, but several hundred people lived here. The village was older, and here there had been a battle in the Civil War, when the White Guards under Mannerheim had advanced to seize Tampere. Here Uncle Matti lived for the moment, though he was still much away from home.

Aarne cried, "There's Uncle Matti!"

Pekka hung on to his elation.

He was a staunch old man, with an outdoor face, standing very still, waiting for us. He was taller, and lankier, than Pekka, and had a dryly deliberate, watchful expression, as though this best met the world. One could not have seen him as over eighty. He didn't budge when we drew alongside, but regarded us for a moment in silence. He wore a lumber jacket and soft knee boots; there was an impression of care about his appearance, and looking again at his face one could see that beneath the seaman and lumberjack and whatever else in his time he had been there was considerable sophistication. It was no surprise, when we went indoors, to find the house lined with books.

He spoke a spare, precise English. No one had mentioned that Uncle Matti knew English; and he, he said, could hardly remember, it was so long ago, when he had learned it. As a sailor perhaps, at the turn of the century, sent to sea to avoid the Russian call-up, for he had already known it in 1904, the year that Bobrikov was shot in Helsinki, the year he himself had gone to Canada. He mentioned Bobrikov as if it had been yesterday, as if these things should always be mentioned, were the natural stuff of one's thoughts; and putting everything else to one side, his waiting and now more solemn nephew, and the others, and his wife, and another young man, he continued in English, rounding off that epoch, that little flow of events in his mind—"There was insurrection throughout the Russian Empire. You will have heard of the battleship *Potemkin?* It led, a year later, to the general strike, in which Finns played their part. That brought about so-called reforms. Here in Finland, in the Grand Duchy, we obtained a single chamber Diet, elected by full adult suffrage. Women for the first time in Europe voted. But the Diet was dissolved. The Tsar preferred terror. It took the Bolsheviks to finish the Tsar. Then the way was opened for our country.

"But has she availed herself of it?" he continued. A rhetorical question, for while I was exulting in having at last found someone who recalled, and enjoyed recalling, the entire span of the century, he had switched off all interest in it, and was devoting himself, in Finnish, to Pekka. It was a chance to glance at the titles on his shelves. Volumes in half a dozen languages. Volumes, notebooks, open on the table. It was a studious house, simple and homely, with here and there a touch of flamboyance that one assumed came out of his wife, for she was much younger, much younger than he, though she also looked a thoughtful person, very sensible and rather comely in her quiet movements in and out of the room. Aarne and Toivo were talking to her and following her with their attentive eyes. She was checking that everything was ready on the table for the opening session of coffee and cake.

Pekka told Aarne to tell me that shortly we should be having a sauna. Uncle Matti had already heated it, so that now it was ripening, as the saying is, the walls, ceiling, platform, and floor taking on an even heat. Too moist or smoky an atmosphere, from a too rapid heating of the stones, would destroy the initial sense of rightness that should fill one on entering the chamber. The pre-sauna mood was already settling on us. Serious talk had to wait until afterwards. There were a few questions about the village and the paper factory. Aarne whispered, "You know, if you want to become a fisherman . . . really it is Uncle Matti who should teach you!" The old man seemed to cast a spell, from his elderly but virile personality, over the quietly waiting menfolk. Pekka for certain was taking it seriously, bending himself with a true modesty to the approaching moment of being naked together. The sauna for him *was* the Church, that in its usual form all his life he had rejected. We were sitting in a growing pre-church hush. The meeting, as Quakers say, was centering down.

Every host imparts his personality to the conduct of his own sauna. Today, under Uncle Matti's aegis, one sensed the respect for traditional detail—as, no doubt, when he wrote a letter, or one of his scathing Communist pamphlets, he wrote it in good clean prose; and the chamber was meticulously free of dust or any preliminary steam on the windows, and the warm water was at the right temperature, and all the equipment stood ready. There was a slight smell of smoke, but that was of the essence of one's initial sense of well-being, lulling one further into the mood. Uncle Matti led us onto the platform. The steaming was applied without excess, found best no doubt through his several decades; and as the sweat poured, and time passed in a silently fraternal, an unemphatic atmosphere, I was seized by the blood brothership created, the closeness that caught up into itself all the formal family ties, during this intimate kind of sauna. This was far removed from a certain grossness to be felt in the Stromfors Company sauna, that day after the football match; and to take a comparison from a different culture, the latter was more like a south Indian temple, at sundown, with the townsfolk doing puja, while the former, the intimate moments now, were reminiscent of a guru praying, alone or with a small group of questioners, under some anonymous tree.

Should one see Uncle Matti as a guru? He belied, in his modest manners so far, the strong family prejudice aroused. Perhaps one should see him as an old campaigner, who through exile and other defeats, had been pared down to a military simplicity. When the cause had failed, there had remained endurance, the natural companion of old men, especially those devoted to politics.

Towards Pekka he was wary, distancing himself, then watching the effect with mischief in his eyes. One could now see Pekka from an older point of view, the doggedly stubborn and serious nephew who had striven so hard for the way through life. Meaning that Uncle Matti had taken it more lightly? Yes, there was the dash of adventurer about him, of the dabbler in avant garde ideas; and there was, as was noticeable once again when, cleansed by the sauna, we returned to the coffee table, the touch of the lover with the much younger wife, who was affectionate towards him, towards whom he was attentive. Quite a different personality, then, from Pekka. Though the younger man had to come to him still, as though indeed he had been a guru, just because he had been present in the Tampere prisons in 1918, when Pekka's father had been shot. Therein lay his power.

They were talking in Finnish. I couldn't follow it. I could only be aware of their personalities emerging in ever-lengthening sorties out of the immediate postsauna fuddle. So far, wide agreement. Enjoyment of each other on the beneficent postsauna plane. Though Uncle Matti was sharpening rapidly, detaching himself from the tendency to blur. *"Vietnamissa"* . . . in Vietnam, was indicative.

He discovered I knew Swedish and made them speak Swedish. He was speaking about Russia's great will for peace, threatened by rash American actions. Pekka, as a Social Democrat, agreed with him, adding that the Demo-

cratic Party, as much as the present Agrarian Government, or any Communist, could respect Russia and deal
with her in Finland's interests. Past distrust had no place
now. The peoples of the Baltic must live together, and if
it was a question of choosing again between Germany
and Russia, he also chose Russia, though not to the point
of being colonized. At that point he would fight again, as
he had fought in 1939.

"And as you fought in 1941?"

"Ah yes, we were tricked into that part of it! Mannerheim and the German Command fixed that. That sort of
thing could never happen again."

"The Mannerheim circle hoped to see Russia reduced
permanently to the size of a second-class power. Do you
think the Soviets should quickly forget it?"

"We have paid. Now it is a different world. As you say,
Russia is a force for peace. Though I think, on second
thought, I must add that generally America helps to keep
her so."

Uncle Matti looked unperturbed by this conclusion.
Why expect anything better from a Democrat?

He said to me in English, as though the thought had
stayed with him and had been joined now by another
group of memories "—Yes, my English was also improved
when I served in the Finnish Legion near Murmansk.
In those days I was not yet a Communist, I called myself a
Finnish Socialist. I was able, you see, to escape from
prison . . . after they had shot my brother. I got away
from Tampere, over the border. There were about two
thousand of us, all Red Guard men; we had fought the
Whites—in this very district. I remember how they forced

us back across the lake near to this house. My brother, by trade he was a printer's foreman, he had become a Company Commander. They were determined to shoot him if they caught him. . . .

"So, at Knaso, on dunes by the White Sea, we were refugees, living in barracks, with little food. Some dying of dysentery. The British were there to guard the area against the Germans using it. The Bolsheviks still trusted the British; and the British backed our side in Finland, because the Whites had German support. As usual, a socially false lineup. But . . . for a time . . . we served the British Force. They formed us into a Finnish Legion to guard that frontier of Russian Karelia against a possible German attack from Finland directed at the Murmansk railway. I was used as an interpreter, and improved my English. Colonel Burton, a Canadian, led us. . . .

"Then, after the German surrender, we were not required any more. But the British, I will say, did stand by us, ensuring our safety when we were returned to Finland. I no longer felt it to be my Fatherland. But I stayed, working for my brother's children. I was among the first Communists in the Diet, though I found the so-called legality a farce in view of the forces that controlled society. The events of the thirties convinced me further. So I remained in Sweden during the war; I did not return to fight for this country."

"But, supposing that Russia had overrun her . . . as with Estonia and Latvia . . . would you have served the occupying force?"

"I would have served the Socialist society that would have followed."

"Bring that evil blood to the surface!"
Lehtikuva Oy

*"Eligible for
the right boys and dances."*

*" 'All those old quarrels . . .' He shrugged. . . .
'We don't talk politics.' "*

"He evidently relished this word 'serfs'
to describe city people."

"Here it was as natural to approve of the factories as in Mecca one would the mosques."

"We are strong, but moderate.
We are men of conscience."
Lekkikuva Oy

"This light and silence is at the heart of Finland."

"To change, that's the problem. . . ."

"We are
a winter people. . . .
Winter
makes strong."
Aarne Piekinen Oy

"The Finns had
the essence of
champion runners."

"Good-bye to the past and
to prayers offered beyond
the grave."

"So do you still support that solution?"

"The time has passed for it. Finland has learned . . . to speed up its internal change."

"You mean it is becoming a Socialist society?"

"We are working to keep it in that direction. We have power now. We are a legal party."

"Many people think that your power is fading."

"How can it . . . in Finland's external situation?" His watchful old face looked wily, bland; the objective reality for him was so patent he did not need to spell it out further. There was no vindictiveness in him, however; the time for that had passed too. Old age, as a Communist on Russia's borders, seemed for Uncle Matti to be quietly satisfactory.

(But they were saying afterwards that he was still a menace, with his pamphlets and lectures to clubs and students, and the summer trips he made to the north, fomenting strikes among the logging community. His wife should control him! For she supported him; she brought him a steady if slender income, derived from a Norwegian hardware store. Her first husband had been a Communist too. What a bourgeois story! Just like Uncle Matti.)

Meanwhile we were attending to a Finnish supper. From the window there was a superb view of the lake—the succession of islets, the wide sky that entered into every moment indoors, so naturally for the Finns that no one remarked on it. They were eating with rather noisy satisfaction, and Uncle Matti had provided wine. He signaled the toasts. That was when we drank. After open sandwiches of salted herring and salmon, the main dish was a creamy mixture of pieces of pork with onion and potato, and to the side a cucumber salad. Then a semolina pudding with figs and cream. What talk there was had reverted to Finnish. Pekka was looking a shade more defiant. Uncle Matti seemed unaware of it.

Immediately afterwards (the food eaten fast, in a half silence, as though we were trekking, were being pursued, and could not allow very long for this snatch of nourishment) we left them together, for their important talk; and Aarne, Toivo, and myself strolled beside the lake away from the village. Well, there were another two houses, then boat houses, then, round a promontory, the village had gone! It had been swallowed by trees. If it hadn't been for the telltale smoke from the paper factory, very black against a misty yellow sunset, we could have felt ourselves lost in the unending forest. There was the semblance of a path. We kept close to the lake, on firm ground ribbed with rocks, till we came to a jetty, half sunk by winter storms and then pinned down by the ice, its two white benches looking oddly elegant and evoking midsummer fantasies. Opposite was the first islet, with a thicket of spruce, just large enough for a hut (the villa) and another hut (the sauna) and between them a miniature man-made cove within which a boat was secured. Smoke curling up from the villa revealed that the owner was there for the weekend, very likely at that moment in his sauna, very likely alone, seeking extra privacy in this very private neighborhood, seeking, as Finns seemed to do, the kernel within the kernel of his thoughts. Brooding in his sauna, alone, silent, in the midst of silent lakes and forests.

It would have been sacrilege to have hailed him.

He would have hated us, conceivably shot at us.

They stared wistfully across at the islet, at that private nirvana. We strolled on. No one talked.

You don't talk much in this immensity of forest. You inhale it, imbibe its drifting moods, its minute variations; and then by the lakes you keep on halting, standing and listening, knowing this to be the very heart of Finland. Whichever spot it is, and with sixty thousand lakes there are billions upon billions of identical spots—just a single protruding rock, say, with the dark water rippling across it, and marsh or a clump of reeds to the side and behind that trees, but in front of you the sky, already changing a fraction since you looked, interchanging with the light on the water, which is a soft-toned light, which could link eternity and all the worlds that have ever been to this particular lakeside moment . . . which is a dominant feeling in the music of Sibelius . . . and informs the painting of Gallén-Kallela, and the writing of Sillanpää and Kivi . . . and is there, the lyrical, the mystical element, in the somber expression of every Finn—this light and silence, caught at the lakeside, whichever spot it is, is at the heart of Finland. You don't have to travel about, in order as it were to accumulate views, so as to understand the country; it is all there by the nearest lake. That lakeside is essentially Finland.

We saw night fall, then strolled back by the glimmer still coming off the water. Lights shining from the group of houses. We had been away two hours; it had not seemed long. The comely Norwegian wife greeted us. She had just been preparing more coffee and pulla.

In the room the atmosphere was the opposite to the

rather ethereal one of our walk. Uncle Matti looked spry, amused, but in a guarded and distanced way. Pekka looked very red in the face. He looked stubborn but as though this had not availed him. There had obviously been outspoken debate. Not a good omen for the success of the visit, intended to cement Pekka's peace of mind with regard to accepting the land offer. He would have done better to have walked with us. Why chance other people's vagaries?

For this, as Aarne joked later, was the trouble. At first there had only been reasonable discussion. Uncle Matti, far from censoring, had encouraged his nephew to accept the land—well, suggesting a little that for one like Pekka, whose life had become so conservative anyway, it hardly mattered at this stage. But this slight acerbity swallowed, an acceptance had been steadily encouraged. Talk had covered all kinds of topics, their best meeting since the war. Why then? Because, toward the end, Uncle Matti— saying it was because he might die at any time, and this disagreement stayed on his conscience (but did it? Aarne queried. Wasn't it more out of a delight in mischief?)— Uncle Matti had told his nephew that he ought to make it up with his sister. Yes, even if she had married a White! Was Pekka the one to be self-righteous? He had suggested that the two of them together should write her a con- ciliatory letter; better, they should telephone her that eve- ning! He, Uncle Matti, would not care to die without making it up with Kirsti. Yes, even if she was hysterically bitter. A start should be made. Didn't Pekka understand that if now, as acceptance of the land betokened, he was entering the most settled period of his life, with old divergent feelings reconciled, he could not omit to make peace with his sister?

In that way the guru had spoken.

Aarne, who was usually so circumspect in referring to any of the family conversations, had felt no stop in relating this one. He had been taken anew by his Great-Uncle Matti. Uncle Matti was a lively old man, with a flexible and adventurous mind. "Politically, perhaps, he is a danger, yes. He says only what he wants you to know. But, within the family, he is a sensible voice. My father, I think, ought to listen to him."

For, of course, for days nothing happened. Pekka being so forthright and honest admitted to his wife the whole conversation (the girls, too, overheard and were discussing it), and she was pleased, but said nothing—for it must have surprised her as much as her husband that the old unrelenting revolutionary should have proposed this particular act of peace. Could it be a Communist maneuver to discredit Pekka among his friends? For all of them approved the stand he had taken, even with regard to his own sister. His sister had been the most awful renegade, had said the most terrible things about the Democrats. It was not uncommon, in cases like this, for the quarrel never to be made up.

If now he accepted the Company land, *and* sought friendship from White relatives with whom as yet he had never spoken, wouldn't that prove too much for his colleagues, for those in the Union who had always grudged his promotion to the rank of manager? Wouldn't it even disturb his own mind, already battling with questions of integrity, to a point where he might become ill? Moral problems weighed heavily on him. They drove him unbearably into himself. So Mrs. Suusanen herself felt suspicious, and counseled him from the opposite view to that which she had formerly maintained; that is, since the idea came from Uncle Matti, not to act hastily upon it.

He didn't. He seemed to do nothing at all. Pekka was more than ever perplexed. In his terribly conscientious mind one could imagine the arguments circling slowly. He sat in the evenings with scarcely a word, while through the window the daylight lengthened and looking at television became less the seasonal thing to do. He had not given his reply to the Company; and now they were all anxious about that, for Mr. Koivaara had warned him that other names were being considered. All of them, even Pekka, by now had come to take the land for granted. But still he couldn't just simply accept, as it seemed to involve this other dilemma.

He was the epitome of the inflexible man, made so by a lifetime of always feeling his actions to be justified.

Uncle Matti had certainly fixed him.

Had it been partly out of mischief, just a little out of professional malice?

For that evening, after we returned and were sitting again round the homely table, with Pekka red and refusing to speak so that his son and Toivo looked utterly bewildered, Uncle Matti had kept the talk going with just a little too much innocence. He was after all too intelligent not to know that he had sowed a new dilemma. Perhaps, as a Communist operating among non-Communists, he saw that as his function, or could not stop himself from doing it in the case of such a solid citizen as Pekka?

Why should Pekka after all not face up to this additional problem? Why should his conscience lie down with the land, if it couldn't lie down with his "White" sister? Uncle Matti saw with military simplicity.

He produced from a drawer, in a way that suggested he always kept this ready for a visitor, a handbill dated 1919. It was a May Day handbill that had been printed in Tampere—"by my brother's mates. It says like this . . . last May Day Finland's bourgeois waded in the blood of our brothers and sisters. That blood cries for revenge. Comrades starved to death in the prison hells. Brothers, sisters, no peace with the bourgeois! Let us answer bayonets with bayonets! Blood for blood! Long live the revolution!"

"A historic document."

"Yes. It shows exactly how we felt at the time. I as you know was still in Russia, but even on May Day 1921 our feelings had not changed in Tampere."

"Have they changed yet? Other Finns accuse you, the Communists here, of deliberately fomenting these old memories, so as to maintain social divisions."

"No. Why should we? We have a policy for the future, that is educational and technological. All Finns, whatever their past, can join us. It is the bourgeoisie who are still suspicious, who exclude us from our rightful positions—in government, in banking, even in industry. A young Communist in Finland, who is not a manual worker, finds the important doors closed to him."

"Despite the proximity of the Soviet Union? Despite what you called the internal evolution?"

"Yes, eventually we shall win our place. But, I assure

you, not by looking to the past. The future, throughout
the world, will be Communist. That is the passion we
give to the young. I have just been saying to my nephew,
your friend, that the past can safely be forgotten. . . ."

But at that point none of us knew what in reality he
had been urging on Pekka. Nor did he himself seem at
all the man to forget past events. Though possibly,
growing older, and with his comely wife, he had found
a basis of reconciliation. He was too complex for one to
guess more about him than that.

He saw us off, standing as before, erect and spare and
guardedly watchful (guarding the flickers of humor in
his face), seeming to sniff the cool night air with pleasure,
testing his old strength against it, and was standing thus
as we took the bend, Toivo again with his skill at the
wheel beginning to demand our concentration. From then
on we watched the road. But at corners, in the lights, I
seemed to see the wily old face of Uncle Matti, the slightly
suspect guru of the Suusanen clan.

6

THE SWEDISH FINNS

I T IS impossible to set down all that happens. One has to choose, to eliminate; and if what remains seems artificial, too carefully chosen for its formal effect—when life, people say, is so haphazard—one can only plead that these events impinged on one as the important ones, and that one has set them down soon after and simply, and that then possibly in the act of writing only relevant sights and smells and gestures and roughly remembered conversation have come off the pen, excluding the rest—the fact that the talk did wander on, about Kennedy, and Maurice Chevalier, or that next evening we went to the cinema, or that people from the factory came for coffee (a rare event), or that personally I was making other friends and ceaselessly discussing Finland with them (some part of which inevitably is filtered back into the Suusanen scenes)—because, unquestionably, the rest fades beside the looming figure of Pekka. Pekka seized by his personal conundrum. Pekka brooding evening after evening, as though a false move between himself and the Company, and then again (just trust it to have come up) between himself and his errant sister, would call his entire life into question. Had he perhaps always seen himself askew, through an image imposed by the previous generation? Or was he just aging, weakening? Who was he? Above all, he must act by principle . . . but which one?

Pekka filled the stage for each of us with whom he was in contact . . . however the talk wandered on. Doing other things only recalled that back in the flat a middle-aged man, even for a Finn very conscientious, was wrestling for the truth—and that this mattered, did reflect his times and country, and that in recording it one didn't seem able to stray far from the bare statement. So, much other industrious information, variant impressions, statistics, and so on, were quietly getting lost as a result. The path for Pekka and his observers was narrow.

Yet at this moment, looking back on Tampere, looking from this summery, idyllic nook, this so differently motivated household (for at last I am staying with Lars in the country), I query that I have drawn Pekka strongly enough. Against the light sophistication here, the weariness of plenitude, he stands in such contrast. He roars from the shadows, each time we play croquet. He throws his shape across my thoughts each time there is the light tinkle of drinks, or with somebody's conduct questioned, when the comment takes to its usual shrug. He stands behind our chairs at dinner wondering why we eat so slowly, why we talk and spin it out. It is not that he envies the comfort or security, backed by investments and ownership of land, for he, like all the middle range of workers, has seen his living standards soar. His Union also owns property and shares. His wife can buy any goods she fancies; there is nothing lacking in the Suusanen flat. It's true, he was short of cash when it came to Helmi's and Aarne's education, but they are doing all right. He bears no resentment. Certainly, their children will go to college. No, his grouse is not economic; he now accepts free enterprise society, stringently checked and taxed by the State; materially speaking, he is as bourgeois as any of them, and this indeed is part of his travail. Affluence has become his right, yet has he been tricked in the process of attaining it?

No, his grouse is not economic; nor that people are idling in the country, for he too is talking of a holiday. He too, like every Finn, would like to sink for a time into the landscape (and with the long winter it is socially permissible to grab every day one can of summer away from the cities and the work routine; no one carps at his neighbor doing that). No—I can feel him breathing down my neck as we sit over wine, and the talk gets excited—it is the play of words and quick abandonment of attitudes, the seeming lack of a serious morality; it's the hedonism that has got him annoyed. Why, in any case, talk so much?

He stalks away from us . . . and I follow him, feeling that as far as Finland goes he is still the more representative, above all among his generation, and that his generation gives the country its character. Only, however many words I use, I doubt that I put across his power, of this fighter reassessing himself.

Two weeks have gone by since I left Tampere, and I suppose I am beginning to think again about it because tomorrow I am returning there. They don't know that I am here, with a Stromfors—worse, with Mrs. Eksberg, the stepmother, twice widowed, of signal strength of mind, who has a signed photo of Goering in the lavatory and remembers him as an interesting gentleman. They think I am traveling in Savo and Karelia, for I set off for Joensuu, and for a steamer trip down Lake Saimaa, the possibilities of which were mapped by the girls, who were relieved to see me becoming a tourist. I shan't be seeing the girls again. I doubt I shall be seeing much more of Tampere. Marjatta is returning. The exchange will be over.

I am glad that my last memory of the girls is such an

exuberant one. It was on the 31st of May, the school closing day, when children listen to the headmaster's sermon and parents attend the end-of-year songs, and a great amount of money has been spent on new dresses and shoes and coats, which is nothing to what, higher up the ladder, at Gymnasium level, is spent on the clothes, with new two-pieces for the girls and sober white-cuffed suits for the boys; and then at the level of our two girls, graduating, being promoted it was called, a thousand marks each (say, one hundred pounds) had been spent on their day and evening wardrobes for the elaborate academic celebrations. They bloomed with all this fantastic expenditure. Finns who usually have to keep an eye on the cost-of-living index go wild in decking out their children for this climax of the educational year. Roses abound. No girl feels feted unless the diploma or title she is receiving is crowned by immense bunches of roses. No one stints. The papers are full of it, and television; it's a national bean-feast. And as another twelve thousand or so white caps appear (and stare for weeks from photographers' windows) every reasonable Finn gives a cheer for this best proof of national progress.

Soon they will be leading the world, proportionately, in the numbers pushed through to college level.

It was a great day; the girls were delirious; roses galore, no one had forgotten them; they could already see themselves in New York, or in outer space, cabling back articles. Rosy futures. A rosy send-off. Pekka nodded and smiled at their happiness as, dressed to the teeth, they went out to a dance. They were good, decent, deserving girls . . . he switched on the set to follow the celebrations in other cities up and down Finland.

He came out of himself generously that evening.

Next day I left for Kuopio, cross-country by train and bus. Whereas in May there had been school excursions packing the trains with studious faces, now from the 1st of June there was an intense and anarchic summer spirit abroad. Individuals, or pals, or gangs, in bright bits of clothing and nylon macs, invaded the carriages, changed seats a dozen times, shared noisily the one magazine, went in their excitement repeatedly to the lavatory, and as the train went clanking, ringing its bell, into each little forest station they rehearsed the panic that was to become a stampede when at last they reached their destinations. Some were going home, from lodgings to their farms; some were already setting off camping, with the minimum of gear, or to the lakeside cabin that was to be their three months' freedom base, where, apart from a few necessities from a farm, all they would need would be a bit of string, to get the outboard motor going, a stout knife, and insect repellent. Parents would be drifting out later with radios and cushions and extra pullovers, but these young pioneers had blazed ahead with little more than went in their pockets. Their feeling of release would keep them warm. Their primitive need to re-enter the forest would blind them to material deficiencies. It was summer (it was not a very sunny day); it was the end to city life and bustle and the beginning of an expansive isolation, and being Finns this was what they went for. Their impatience to arrive was almost hysterical.

The train shed them, and took on others, but the bus for the last stage to Kuopio appeared to be still a season behind, carrying day workers home, each of them as he left the bus returning his ticket to the driver-conductor (against waste, litter? A final check on honesty? A proof to one's fellows of one's right to leave the bus?); and Kuopio itself, building, expanding with model plans above lake and forest, was too busy becoming a city to bother much about June having struck. In any case it was circled by lakes, lake breezes blew from every quarter, across islets with beaches and outdoor restaurants, and a harbor so dense with holiday craft, among which towered the double-decker steamers, that one could see the whole population at whim taking to the water, disappearing, between the end of office say and midnight or in the hours before breakfast, weighing anchor, and scattering through the maze of channels and inlets each to some life-sustaining hideout; so here perhaps more patience was possible before the big summer plunge began.

For even from here there would be an exodus, from these lakes and forests to remoter lakes and to forests where fewer people trod, the ideal being, as Finns half joked, to find a retreat where at least for a fortnight no other human would intrude his presence. There would only be you there, and God. God would wrap you about with his silence, and his sunshine, and his primeval creation. It was getting more difficult, however, these days. More roads, more inquisitive traffic. And so much wilderness ceded to Russia.

A day alone was becoming a triumph.

Rather counter to this mood overtaking Finns at the onset of their summer, I was rapidly feeling too much alone. The Suusanen household, however austere, and despite the continuing barrier of language, had been my nest; one got used to nests, and there I had felt drawn into the tension that, consonant with winter perhaps, had held them during recent months. I was rapidly missing it. I thought only about it as trains and buses swayed and scudded through the remoter parts of Savo and Karelia. I had imagined it would be interesting to return to Joensuu where we had worked with war evacuees. Not at all. It was a draughty market town, with commercials crowding the hotel bars, and the streets flitting with ghostly teen-agers, who stared through the windows at sewing machines and refrigerators and agricultural machinery, or occasionally changing posts at the main corners, seemed to be passing a message around, perhaps to do with an interplanetary future, or with some lost childhood scene. They bothered me, these phantom creatures, the girls especially thin and waiflike, in shabby trousers and ex-service jackets, alone or in whispering haunted groups; as if indeed they had been survivors, not just of the war that I remembered, when their families could have been pitched in here en route from farms in eastern Karelia to wherever else in Finland could be found for them, but of some more deadly unseen war, that had killed off everyone over twenty—for to them the adult world in view, in cars, on the pavement, in the matronly cafés, appeared not to exist. They saw beyond it. They saw only each other. They flitted for a time, then suddenly were gone.

The same in Savonlinna, in Lappeenranta. Indoors, in hotels and *ravintolas*, the middle-aged, middle-class jollity prevailed, where money brought the starched-white waitress with a tray of heavy food and drink, and the orchestras played their old-fashioned jazz, and the dancers trod on each other's toes. But outside, in the squares, in doorways, most markedly at eleven when the cafés closed, the younger generation fitted; and though some at the hot-dog stalls were noisy and even a little threatening, the majority were of the hushed variety, as though voice, in an automated world, would be just another point-less attribute; and they flitted for a time, then faded down side streets.

To some extent I had seen them in Helsinki, and in Turku, and, infrequently, in Tampere (in Tampere every-thing was more robust, more notched to the nonstop factory flywheel), and I supposed that they were more in evidence now, weather apart, because in these eastern provinces of Finland the industrialized economy of the future had not yet found a place for them. They knew about it, and that nothing else sufficed, so they were hang-ing about in the wings, waiting. Yet against this notion stood the memory of the scene current in central Stockholm —surely the most advanced, most wealthy Nordic center, where these same lost youngsters flitted, in tiny groups but by the hundreds, wearing the same outcast uni-form, looking unearthly, in the thrall of distant forces, as they were blown almost, hither and thither, between the rich white skyscrapers and the glass-lined shopping corridors. There they too had appeared not to see you, by your dress so obviously over twenty, by your step so bound to the visible world. Who were they, these Nordic phantoms, their number greatest in the wealthiest metrop-olis but present also in Finnish market towns?

Were they rejecting our material culture?

Did even their humanity seem redundant?

They didn't lift the loneliness of travel, and what with the rain over Lake Saimaa, and the chilliness that kept returning when now the sky should be blazing with heat, I scurried west again to Helsinki. My opinion is that for the fisherman or camper who seeks a solitary nature-bound holiday, then the lakes and forests of Finland will rejoice him; there as in few parts of Europe today he can catch the authentic ring of solitude, he can ponder his ephemeral condition against the everlasting wheel of the seasons—for Finland evokes this kind of thinking. But if he's a tourist, an antiquity collector, a motorist who expects some local custom or meal or constant change in the landscape to blazon each of his days as remarkable, then better go south, to the Latin south, or if he has the money, go east, young man.

Lars met me in Helsinki. He was back from Tenerife, waving penny-a-time cigars, talking of shots of brandy for sixpence. It was wonderful to hear it. One's world flooded back.

That afternoon we motored to the country, to his stepmother's boyar-styled manor house.

"Lars," I asked him, "do you still have influence in the Stromfors Company?"

He smiled his old self-deprecating smile, the first hour of our encounter enabling him to link up with his former self. He liked this; for though he looked fit, bronzed and active, slightly underweight, there were shadows in his face that had become a part of its texture, that bore no relation to youthful anxiety. Our encounter superimposed old attitudes. "You know, my dear friend, that I never had that. They wrote me off as a medical fellow. A nihilist, my uncle called me." But he would be using a phrase of his father's, picked up thirty years before. The Stromfors family were not imaginative.

"They built a cathedral in the shape of a sauna."

"Ah yes. You've tried it? I'm not keen on saunas. You must tell me what you've been up to in Tampere."

"Well, it all comes to this. . . ." I enlarged on Pekka, ending with this latest dilemma that threatened to lose him the land, even now, if it led to much further hesitation. Could Lars get through to his Tampere cousins to ensure that the offer was extended indefinitely?

"You've not called on them, have you?" He smiled ironically, tempering it with his unchanging courtesy. Unchanged also was his immaculate appearance, the slightly overdone fastidiousness. "It would not have been fair on Suusanen, would it?" His smile lengthened. He too had caught himself sliding back into that favorite attitude.

"Oh, but I haven't changed. . . ." He brushed it aside. "Yes, I think I can get that point over to them. They probably know it. It is Welfare nowadays that keeps the factory wheels turning! I shouldn't worry, they are probably so hurt by Suusanen's indifference to their bounty . . . they will end up by offering more. How all that has come full circle!

"You know," he went on in a different tone, "before I gave up my practice, I was getting an increasing number of patients from among the higher brackets of workers. Men like Suusanen, who were into middle age, and still racing up the industrial ladder. They had nervous fatigue. They even hated the pace. Yet all they wanted were pills, pills especially, so as to give them more application. So as to earn more, spend more, acquire bigger debts!"

"Yes, but Pekka isn't at all like that."

"No? I'm glad. Or he'd end up in hospital. Not that that ever changed my patients. They came out, and continued as before. They would not face an inner reappraisal.

"You know," and again his tone varied slightly, "you could say now that I am generalizing. But I increasingly believe we must lose ourselves, and that this is the lesson for the second half of life. I am putting it generally—whoever we are. Up to forty we are finding ourselves, whatever our role or circumstances, we are weaning our particular shape free. Then, no sooner done, we ought to lose it. We should change what is constant back to a variable and stand our old lives on their heads. That would give freedom—or call it health—to throw away what we set most store by. Perhaps automation will give us the push to try out two or three lives in one."

"Not a bad plan. But surely here in Finland, with the weekly sauna and the forest and so on, the pressures are less, a man stays freer?"

"Quite wrong, my dear friend. Those are used to sustain him in the very role he ought to discard. They are palliatives, straws to clutch at—yes, even the forest as it's used today. Take Tapiola, and such model estates, with the skyscrapers set among the trees: that is no less than the enslavement of Nature to man's obstinate view of himself! To the proud personality he embroiders the more through it. We have been too thoroughly dragooned by the century, and the requirements of affluence. Yes, even

in Finland, even in the forest. It is in no way a help if
we are going to change. It's better to take the strain without palliatives. To change, that's the problem. . . ."

"Well, for all of us, the second half of life . . . is a
bit of a teaser. What should be aids are usually contami-
nated. But, listening, Lars . . . forgive me for asking,
but is this particularly about yourself?"

"Hah! Very likely." He fell silent, attending to the
road. Lars drove like an Englishman, with caution and
consideration. He was no Toivo. His shining Mercedes
entered no contest with anyone else. Like the countryside it provided him a background for talk and friendship and the self-appraisal that, for him certainly, was
the anchor of existence. In the last few minutes his features had relaxed. The shadows had lightened, though
not to disappear.

"So I don't suppose you are an advocate of *sisu?*"
Sisu is a Finn's much lauded quality of guts and endurance to the point of invoking the gods themselves for
the job in hand. *Sisu* always achieves the impossible. Lars
had certainly upheld it in wartime.

"Up to twenty-five, I do admire it. After that, consider-
ing the pride it gives rise to, I would say a man was better
without it. It was indispensable to youthful Finland. Today Finland needs other virtues. One always sees it in
politicians; they are mesmerized by their unfailing *sisu*.
Like their erotic powers. All nailed to the mast."

"I see. One has to discard all?"

"Well, put it that way, but it's not so simple. I suppose
I had better admit at this point that I am thinking of
entering the Catholic Church. I saw that I should, in

Tenerife." His fine long face shone momentarily, the
furrow in the center of his forehead straightening. The
hair that had once been full and golden was silvered
and thinly brushed back. His eye was very steady on the
road. "You know, of course, that we were a Catholic country, in the wake of Sweden, from the twelfth century. Our
patron saint was Henry, an Englishman, martyred
here by suspicious peasants. It's a great pity that the
Lutheran Church ever came to these northern countries.
Think how much jollier we should have been without
it!"

"I see that the south has been undermining you. It
does that to Englishmen too."

"Yes, though if we have to be fair, Finns have so
divided into sects and dramatized their religious feelings
that Luther would hardly know his own."

"I always thought that you were agnostic."

"I was. It's part of what I'm discarding." He paused
for a time. "I suppose you will try to explain all this
to me in social terms. . . . I am a Swedish Finn . . .
in full retreat . . . Rome is one of the options left to
me, as the majority forces wash me under. Something
like that?"

"I wouldn't presume to."

"Oh yes, but I talk like that! I devil it out from every
angle." He laughed, and slowed as we entered a village.
Lohja. "I want to show you the church here. Medieval.
Frescoed walls. The most beautiful buildings in Finland,
before Aalto, are a few of these medieval churches." Inside, after an impartial inspection, he knelt in one of the
pews to pray.

We drove on to the manor in silence.

However, whatever was brewing in Lars, in his grappling with the Nordic complexities of existence, toward his stepmother, and the other guests who came in that evening for dinner, he showed an impeccably urbane front. Mrs. Eksberg, tall, big-boned, with a crisply withering sense of humor wrapped up in formality of manner, kept challenging him, by implication, to say what was really on his mind, but smiled commending him when he turned the question. They kept on trying to charm each other, and obviously had a good understanding. Drink flowed. The talk waltzed about. "A peasant girl," as Mrs. Eksberg called her—that is, a country Finnish Finn, with face and hair like Sophia Loren's—saw to the drinks and a tray of canapés, then clocked out on the stroke of six, to be collected by a local sawmill engineer, to be driven down to Hangö for the evening. Sometimes he took her as far as Helsinki. That made her, in Mrs. Eksberg's view (who naturally referred to the capital as Helsingfors), into a motorized peasant.

Over drinks another girl looked in, a summer neighbor's daughter, who was a familiar of the house. I must describe her: she was a big-eyed blonde, with dark eyebrows, and loose, long hair. She was reading law, but now on vacation turned up in faded jeans and a black string top and kick-off sandals. She was full of temperament, her fluent body a ball she was eager to throw into play, so long as Lars was also playing. For she was set on him. He parried easily, and seemed flattered, not disturbed. She roared off to change, in an open sports car, the throb like her heart's determined excitement persisting across the copses and orchards and the birch and ash-lined inlets of the sea, silencing all the summer birds; and returned wearing a short white dress, that darkened her skin and made her look sixteen. We had also changed and were sitting on the terrace, like grandees, for though she called it a cottage our hostess had a miniature fortress here, and the drinks were gently flowing again. The sun was setting in a blaze over Sweden. In Lapland you could already see it all night.

We were joined for dinner by an officer of the old school, in mufti he would term it, of clarion opinions, who had a great respect for English life (I think, of the pre-Beatles era), and little use for the lesser breeds or for anyone who went into politics, but who for the art world had a covert admiration. He was a watercolorist. He had a feeling for materials. His eye rested on the table service and the lamp fittings and on a stoneware pot that filled one end of the sideboard opposite as though these simple beautiful objects contained exactly what had eluded him, in battle as well as at the easel. He pressed the girl Monica to tell him about the views of her generation. His eyes were expressive toward her also. While she turned everything into a half-impassioned appeal to Lars.

Everything in the room was well chosen and subordinated to a spaciousness that bounced off the white roughcast walls and flowed about the dining area, between the light birch table and the dark flower-painted sideboard, a Karelian piece once bought in Viipuri, and through a door to a passage and the kitchen quarters; and flowed through an arch to the main living area with its low leather settees and coffee tables, and plants, and wall shelves, and Dutch-tiled stove; and through a door there to a heated loggia with a profusion of plants and wicker chairs, and tall tables, and from there to the terrace; and in all this vista what reclaimed one's eye, time and again among the other objects, was a tall willowy Ostrobothnian clock. There were so many things if one's eye rested, as the Captain's did, as it were for inspiration, of old pewter and glass and wood, though in the main, as our hostess had considered it her duty to patronize modern Finnish crafts-men, Winkkala and Franck for her glass and pottery, Lisa Johansson-Pape and Nummi for her lighting, the ground floor had a contemporary look. Upstairs, with her Biedermeyer boudoir and Gustavian bedroom, and corridor of portraits, historical perspective was more in evidence.

On the dinner table, the present center of attention, with all those other objects purring in the soft spacious-ness beyond us, and a night breeze just reaching from the terrace, there were strings of flowers at the center and the corners, intended only to last while we ate, and these gave a delightful fragrance. There was still "a peasant" to wait upon us, an old dame who had always been with the family, who as a girl had had the most pretty feet and for that reason had been engaged, as in those days she had served barefoot in the house in the style current in the Russian empire. In fact Lars confessed to a country uncle who still lived in the Tsarist way, not too aware that serfdom had ended; but such people were curiosities in Finland. He had been famous for a few orgiastic parties, but all that was hushed up now.

The food seemed to be wholly Swedish—the most

fabulous smorgasbord, with every kind of herring, anchovies, salmon (smoked and poached), stuffed eggs, sliced meats, ham and asparagus, pickled salads, then a cheese tray, and hot meatballs. Enough to dine on, with schnaps and beer; but Swedish Finns, like their Swedish forebears, seemed to possess warrior appetites, so after a soufflé, there were loin of pork, stuffed with prunes, with red cabbage, all sharp and spicy to taste, then melon and a sorbet. We sat afterwards in the loggia, smiling at a bottle of Remy Martin.

"This country's living beyond its means," the Captain was saying. "Has done for years. Not what Mr. Micawber would approve of!" Like all of them he was speaking in English, a politeness towards their foreign guest. My Swedish was unthinkable here. "Nothing to choose between the parties. People in power enjoy spending money, which increases their scope and again their power. A world bureaucracy is coming into being. Wars are declining. There will be one system, spending what we earn for us. It's misleading to think this is only in Finland; our affairs are fixed by international bureaucrats. Even our debts, I would guess!"

"Aren't you a patriot any more, Captain?" Mrs. Eksberg was a great patriot, even more than Lars roused to distinguish between her group of Swedish Finns and the Swedes of Sweden, who were stuffy cousins. She was nothing but a Finn, of its ruling breed. "Haven't we something unique to contribute?"

The Captain thought. "I'm puzzled to name it. We used to have, as a frontier people, holding the line against the East."

"Very well, then, we are unwavering fighters—like the

British! Though we are fitter than they are. We are practical, a compulsively open-air folk . . . you cannot define us without mentioning our landscape, our arctic winters—so, there it is; we are still a kind of frontier people. We enter the scene, wherever it may be, with a rim-of-the-world freshness to offer."

Lars laughed. "You make us sound like Tibetans! Is that how Americans described our lumberjacks, drinking and pulling knives on their mates? Finns had a vicious reputation."

"Oh, lumberjacks! The peasants still hack one another to pieces with axes. In the backwoods. It doesn't get to the papers. My dear Lars, they are simply peasants. . . ."

"From whom all else proceeds . . . including, usually these days, the President."

"Lars, you know, you are joking," said the girl, perhaps hoping that he would a bit more. It was a soft sweet night. The garden beckoned.

Lars asked me, "Have you heard of Rolf Arnkil?"

"I met his widow, now in Kuopio, and her fine English-Finnish sons."

"That's a good mixture," pronounced Mrs. Eksberg— "English and Finnish, for the men of the future. So long as we keep away from the Latins!"

Lars smiled to himself. "I will lend you his books, if you think you can manage the Swedish. Especially the first, *Inför de ytterska frågorna*. A remarkable man, dying of cancer, yet preserved unexpectedly for three years. This book records his correspondence with two other men, Eskola and Sirenius. It shows him to be a frontiersman, but between man and God, between life and death, between unbelief and Christianity. You've made me recall him, talking of frontiers . . . because, Captain, even if the bureaucrats control our daily affairs increasingly, we are still left with the most important decisions. It's true, as you say, that our being Finns will cease to define us as it used to do, but we shall still be men. It's a liberation. We can focus better on fundamentals."

"If we are already of a certain age. I doubt young people care much." The Captain smiled at Monica invitingly. "It's a good time, isn't it, for you people?"

Her long brown legs pointed from her dress. "I should hope so, Captain." She was responding to him, perhaps hoping to set Lars on edge.

Lars surveyed us all equably.

It could have become an awkward juncture, for the girl looked also ready to sulk, so impatient was she of any restraint, yet held for the moment by Mrs. Eksberg's presence; so that lady, perhaps for reasons of her own, suggested we go boating down the mirror-calm inlet whose waters reached to the foot of the garden. There were patches of mist obscuring the first islet and the neighboring rosemary-scented headland; the reeds stood black against the silver-shining water that looked like lake but was in fact sea. It was warm, seductive. There were a couple of dinghies. Mrs. Eksberg came talking with the Captain, but then decided she would not join us. By then Lars and Monica had gone, their oars plashing fifty yards ahead. With less than a true soldier's philosophy, the Captain tetchily signed to me to row.

He darkly examined each crevice of the mist.

You could hear Monica's mischievous laughter, but

from where? The prongs of land seemed to bar us. It was tricky, finding the right way through, and as soon as I could I grounded the boat.

He accepted defeat; it was just a summer evening, and he turned intently to a discussion of painting. We sublimated, with another form of beauty.

On our return we found that the peasant, the old dame, had prepared more coffee, and was offering to rustle up pancakes if desired. She and her mistress were chatting closely, two cronies, who in their day perhaps had both been admired for their exquisite feet.

Their confidential eyes.

Their pleasure in the evening: that did not contradict their view of life.

Today is Thursday, and my last day here, and since lunch I have been sitting in this waterside arbor with its fringe of nasturtiums and tiger lilies, jotting impressions, perhaps piecing them together into an over-formulated picture—because, after all, where tendencies abound as they do in any social group it is partly chance or one's predisposition that determines which one sorts out.

Better, some say, just to list the contents of the view, or the room, or the national history—as Mr. Gradgrind in *Hard Times* . . . "what I want is facts . . . facts alone are wanted"; but that surely would be equally subjective, because of the cast and rhythm of words that insidiously project the writer. Empathy is as honest an approach, shaping its own verbal equivalent for the reality that of course outreaches it.

Though what is reality? Are there any constants?

This is Lars's influence, his feeling about life, about one's own life and having to lose it, to stand it on its head in midcareer. Though he has retired, he is a retired doctor; he hasn't faced this problem while running. He has already lost interest in the world, in Finland, and this morning he was adding in the whole chapter of Western history. He is seeking another ground for take-off. (A twitch of eyebrows—and what about Monica? He smiles. Monica is a summer's evening. As he for her. They have Nordic detachment.) He keeps saying, "We witnessed the last war. Or, if there is still to be China against the rest of us, that means no way forward was possible. We are stuck with useless minds and bodies. We can't change. It's all up with us."

I notice he keeps varying his depth of view—from his middle-aged self to mankind's dilemma.

But perhaps each of us reflects the whole.

Lars otherwise is fit. Swims like a porpoise. Races to the islets. He is building a boat. He has discovered that he owns some further out island, and there, once he can reach it in his boat, he intends to construct a circular studio. He doesn't pretend the studio is relevant—indeed, he holds to the opposite view; but these activities are an exercise that encourage what's going on in his mind.

We continued talking about the war, till called for lunch—which, being a Thursday, reminded us with its pork and pea soup of the galvanized stockpots of the forest kitchens, and of our uncritical hunger then—

and it was nostalgic, like recalling childhood games: war the last great tremor of childhood; and I reminded him of what he had said concerning the basis of Finland's independence. . . .

"You still remember?"

"I've been digging in my diary. The war was so clearly your country's watershed. Civil strife before, unity since. You said that social and political unity would be the minimum for continuing independence."

"Yes. And I would say that we have exceeded our target. Don't be fooled by factional bickering. Unity has grown out of sacrifice, and legislation, and the habit of parley. All politicians now struggle for the center. Young people expect solutions in the way they expect cars to run. We've made it rather quickly—in part thanks to Russia. She is still there, though Leningrad nowadays is where we go for a few extra drinks! Possibly we serve her as a diplomatic counter in her dealings with the northern arm of NATO, though there again, sanity will prevail.

"Frankly," he went on, "it's trivial today to pretend that Finland has serious problems. We advance, as the Captain said, bureaucratically, helped one month by officials in Moscow, the next by officials in London and Washington. We are outside the main areas of contention, in Asia and Africa. We only read about the issues, or send a few Finns there as patrolmen. Our story gets duller. In fact, Finns, as equally the English, should devote half their time and money to caring for those who are really at the center of the world's material and spiritual perplexities. Well, we don't, do we?"

"You personally are trying to understand something

that concerns everyone. Part of humanity has to turn inward."

"Oh, I'm just an escapist Swedish Finn! As a doctor I ought to be in Johannesburg, or Calcutta, or an Andean Republic. Schweitzer understood. We must live within our century, responding to its most urgent demands. And this century is speeding up fast. It leaves most of us out of date.

"Especially," he added, "we egocentric Finns."

Then the younger of the peasants called us to the terrace. Mrs. Eksberg had completed her morning. Lunch was ready. There was a chill dry hock. Lady and escorts disposed to conversation. The view, arranged, as it should be, for gentlefolk.

Still a very Chekhovian picture.

Within which this arbor fits, and the currents of the sea soft as on a millpond, and the sleepy summer afternoon.

7

LAKESIDE

I RETURNED to Tampere with mixed feelings. The crush and heat in the train seemed designed to recall the leisured house I had left, with its sea-cooled rooms and orchard views. This was not the season to be returning to a city. Pekka would still be worrying his problems. I might have helped him there; of course, I'd have to conceal that I had been anywhere near the Stromfors clan. Just like returning home to my father, always pretending something else. But what struck me most was that in the last few days, through talk and a new turn of ideas, the compulsion that had first brought me to Tampere—to see how a particular Finn had fared in the quarter century since I had carried him in an ambulance—had faded away. It had been displaced. To be returning to the Suusanens made me feel awkward. What had been so natural no longer seemed so. A link, predominantly with the past, had snapped. Perhaps Pekka was feeling the same.

So why go back now?

Small heart. Small fickle traveler's heart. Having said so often that these Häme people were like Yorkshire people but even more so, how imagine that they could have changed?

They hadn't. Within minutes, I hadn't, either.

They were kinder than ever, on their cautious faces the most ready of welcoming smiles appearing. They at once said why. Marjatta was in Helsinki, and had phoned praising her stay in London. She would be coming to Tampere, but not just yet, as she had duties at a summer school at Lappeenranta. Parents must wait, smiled Mrs.

Suusanen, her whole person a study in patience. I told them I had just come from Lappeenranta. "Oh, what a shame! You could have told her how it is there. Hey, hey! Please, ring her now."

But Marjatta, back in her Helsinki flat, smoothing away the last traces of tenants, jumping, one could imagine, with the excitement of travel that she would also see as adding a title to those already before her name, Marjatta, pulsing with her need to express this, in those split seconds was herself on the phone. Mrs. Suusanen knew it. "That will be Marjatta." To me, "You answer. That will give her a surprise."

"Hello, Marjatta."

There was a volley of Finnish, like a lifeline rocketed across one's person; then she understood, and there was some confusion because unthinkingly I had called her "Marjatta." "Miss Suusanen, how nice to greet you," I corrected. "No; yes; Marjatta's okay." She tumbled into a description of my children, of London, of all the work she had accomplished, on a rising, breathless paean that ended with things she had bought on the last day at Selfridge's. A dip of confusion. (Boasting? Not mannerly? The things she had bought were somehow indelicate? Presents—forgotten, or they now seemed redundant?) For seconds a gulf of silence interposed. Then she was speaking again, vibrating but careful to cut out the self-esteem, enquiring about Tampere, saying, "I must warn you, my Aunt Kirsti has been taken very ill. It could even be a mental affliction. My father especially . . . I think you will realize. Please say things to reassure him. He holds you in the greatest respect." Good heavens, the sweet note that corners one, that particularly that day made me feel a worm. Poor Pekka, the final twist of the screw. . . . "Yes," she was saying, but her volubility had by now carried her far beyond, "I wanted to kiss the soil of my country. I hadn't quite the pluck at the airport. You cannot imagine how much I love Finland. I have dreamed of its forests. I am in pain without them"—her speed of talk was like Toivo's driving—"so could you do that thing for me?"

"I'm sorry. I didn't. . . ."

"Oh, that's all right. By the way, you must stay with my family as their guest. My mother insists. Could I speak with her a minute? You will ring tomorrow?"

A heady prospect. Like roller-coasting. But I was never to learn the favor she had asked me. Her mother had taken over the receiver and they continued for some time clocking up the Finmarks, in the way that Finns unconcernedly do.

Pekka had meanwhile left the flat. I had been deceived by his smile, not to notice his misery. There was an empty beer glass on the table. From my room I could see him crossing to the bus stop, and I wondered if he was going to the sauna to sweat some of his cares away.

Shortly afterwards, Mrs. Suusanen confided, knowing very well that I knew of their affairs, and her view was that no blame at all at any time could be laid against Pekka, and that he burdened himself too much for others. "He has always been this way. He is a soldier in every good person's cause. And some less good; they have taken advantage. In the factory, he has been a man of principle. Conditions have changed, so he worries anew. It

is as if he had to rewrite the Bible. I am pleased that
the Company has recognized his worth."

"So your land is safe?"

"There was a time," she went on, "when they thought
he was becoming a politician. I was always against that.
He is an engineer. He may lack the title, but he knows
the work. His Union friends thought he should stand for
the town. His character has always been known locally.
But he preferred to keep his fights within the Company,
and they at last gave credit for that. Now his son, Olavi,
who should become a professor and keep to his university
career, threatens to take the opposite course. What a
pity!" *Vilken synd!* Her smile broadened, as though
bending beneath a weight of aches. "No," she paused
again, "that land has been apportioned. Perhaps later
there will be a new offer to us. But it is God's will. My
sister-in-law calls us, and we cannot think about ourselves.
We are not for the moment taking our holiday. So I
have asked Aarne, I wanted to tell you, to run you out
to Olavi and Anna. There is our room there, that we wish
for you. So that you should know something of our summer by the lake. . . ."

I pressed her to explain. This renewed kindness batted
away at my sense of ingratitude. She was so pleased to
be giving, to be substituting someone else's pleasure for
her disappointments. One could only thank her (and silently pledge not to turn some future beggar from the
door) and protest that as I hadn't yet met Olavi it might
seem to them an awkward intrusion.

"Oh yes, Aarne will take you out fishing. Tomorrow he
has arranged a day free." She showed that the point had

already been discussed. "If then they invite you, then you must stay. Prepare some clothes. Aarne will run back for them." But if they didn't invite me? A small-scale test, that even in moments of gloom and crisis one could see that this Finnish family enjoyed. Will he measure up? Will embarrassment defeat him? The sort of points they liked to know about each other. In even allowing me to enter these lists they were showing how far they had come to accept me.

How distant now were early impressions! Even in the streets a melancholic face, surly and wrapped up in itself, seemed less typical; for one had also learned of the kindness and humor and vitality that abounded. The picture now would be harder to draw. Could a champion runner ever be a misogynist? The Finns had the essence of champion runners.

She began to tell me about Anna, that Olavi had met her at the University, where she worked now as one of the librarians. Not a good plan, because of the child. When a mother worked, her children suffered. Finnish women, so advanced people said, among the most "liberated" in the world, were slowly facing up to this truth. On the farms it didn't matter; but, for instance, factories weren't farms. Each of her children had been left to sleep and play in the Company crèche; the Company had always been so considerate—and was for its employees from cradle to grave—but one understood why. And motherhood suffered.

She was sorry that Anna clung to her career.

Anna was very clever, had published some poetry.

Yes, they had a copy of the book somewhere. (Not previously mentioned. Not visible on the shelves. That Helsinki couple hardly ever referred to. Olavi quoted occasionally for his scholarship, and his views of America, where he had lectured for a year. General impression of his having "climbed" on to some higher social platform, and that this was resented. Note Aarne's attitude. Impression that he was the least devoted of the children; even while in England Marjatta had sent postcards, while now, on the phone . . . though good Mrs. Suusanen, good in every way, clung in her tone to him with equal gratitude.)

She was saying that the land by the lake was Anna's, bought by her father in one of his deals. It was surprising . . . in 1940 he had been a refugee, driven out of Viipuri by the Russians . . . but by 1950 he had built up a business, a very flourishing one, in prefabricated housing. He lived in Lahti. It was full of Karelians. One heard that he was always buying up forest. There had been a court case. He had won it, but people had talked a lot at the time.

He was a lively man—an Orthodox Christian. She had only met him on three occasions.

Was Anna like her father?

Oh no. Perhaps a little. There was something different about Karelian families. Häme people found them difcult to follow. They said the same about people in Häme. Of course, both were Finnish. Yes, Anna, perhaps, had inherited the Karelian changeability. I must not be surprised, or in any way hurt, if at moments . . . it was difficult to explain, but she had felt that she must warn me . . . if at times Anna got very depressed, antagonistic even . . . no harm was meant.

No. (I had imagined that morose depression was a Häme characteristic—say, a winter facet of the many things to be learned about Häme; but here was the most charitable of persons imputing it to a rival strain in the nation!) "Are her poems about depression?"

"I believe, some of them. I think she has had terrible experiences." There was no move to look for the volume.

"Is the child a boy?"

"Pentti? Yes. I hope later to come and play by the lake with him."

"You are very kind to me, to let me go there."

"You are my husband's friend." *Min man's vän.*

Again this unexpected tribute. I had been their lodger, there was a memory from the war, but no very open strings drawing us closer over the previous three months. Then I bethought myself—it was like this in Yorkshire; there too the unspoken, secret maturing of friendship, no matter how slight the beginning, so long as a moral kinship was felt. That vexed word! But northerners understood it, understood the way they liked to use it; and Pekka, simply because I had been there during his critical period for him, must have felt (there being nothing to the contrary) that silently I was offering moral support. I hope, in a northern way, that I had done.

Aarne's idea of an early start was four o'clock in the morning. He had been studying late the night before, after his mother and father had gone to bed, and the table was still littered with his papers. Drawings of wheels, pulleys, magnets, page-long calculations; his face from sleep was equally protracted as though from thermo-dynamic dreams. He woke me up. I followed to the shower. By then he had the coffee going. Toast for the English-man, sausage for the Finn. As I downed a healthy glass of milk I noticed he was checking his wicker creel that like a schoolboy he kept with his slide rule and records, to make sure the maggots, etc., were there. "Don't they ever get out?" "Not usually. I secure them." In a bottle he also had other grubs, decomposing larvae, snails, worms, that rather than throw as final ground bait he had brought home for observation. A bait jar was ready for minnows. He had his fly book and tackle case, ready to suit the progress of the day. He turned from these to prepare our sandwiches, of ham and cheese and egg. We were off.

No conversation on this run out. We streamlined, close to the machine. A lorry or two hurtled down the roads, a taxi with returning revelers, an occasional jeep starting from a farm; for the rest we had the run to ourselves, so fast I was even scared to cry out. I felt like howling as we slithered round corners, the skid just held in control. Trees semaphored, houses burst upon us like sonic bangs; a change of gear, we were gone. The landscape was mostly curling with mist, thick and white at the border of the lakes. Straight ahead, to the north, the sun was shining, a tangerine orb through smoky clouds, then gleaming gold where the sky turned blue. Further north, in Lapland, where the light was constant for seventy days of brilliant daytime, in contrast to the permanent dusk of winter, farmers (as shown us on television) were farming and ditching and repairing their buildings with untiring zeal round the twenty-four hours. Even in Tampere, as we had left, the cleaners had been up and about, cleaning the streets. But here through the mists of the Häme country the summer day was more gently beginning.

If only we could approach it slowly! But Aarne seemed to feel no disconnection between a race on the bike and the tranquility of fishing. Perhaps he was blotting out his studies.

To our right stood Näsijärvi, from Tampere in the south to Virrat in the north—the Poet's Way, as the girls had encouraged me to discover by going on a steamer trip—and it was fed by a hundred south-flowing rivers, each with lakes like beads on a chain, and this constant though pace-varying movement of water was important not only for timber floating but for the fisherman planning how to catch his fish. As we parked the bike by the bend of a river, broadening with fast and slow reaches, and just below where it flowed from a lake, a small lake, a tarn one might call it in recognition of the surrounding hillocks, Aarne began debating, aloud for my benefit, what the trout would be up to along the different banks. He was familiar with the terrain. It depended on the season, on the day, on the wind, on other people's fishing, as to how he could best approach the job. "On other people?" I queried innocently. "One feels to be in the wilderness here." "Oh no"—and as he spoke, from Näsijärvi, a few miles of forest away, came the shattering coughs of an outboard motor erupting into the morning air. A moment later it was snarling evenly. "The villas are packed along Näsijärvi. Plenty of people look about for fishing. On many stretches of river they must pay. Not here—our good luck, but theirs also. The trout are not the size they used to be."

He fitted me out with a ten-foot rod, that waggled freely and seemed well balanced, and a reel line of fine nylon, to which, measuring, he fixed a float and some split-head weights and at the end the hook. To the hook he attached a piece of worm. "Just there," he directed, where the water ran swiftly—"plenty of minnow. Good feed for trout. Throw the line in, or practice your casts. I think, every time you catch something." He showed me where I could dig for mudworms. He was laughing to himself. It was a cool soft morning. Minnows I had to put in the jar. Round the river bend, where the current slackened, if I softly cast always just upstream, I might at this hour of the day catch roach. "Remember, at the first clear movement of the float, to strike, with an upward flick of the wrist. Better too soon than too late, maybe."

My orders received, I still loitered, to watch him knot the gut to his line, and a team of flies he would try on the lake, near the outflow to which the feed brought the trout. He was still talking about the holidaymakers, in between the angling advice. "My brother Olavi, I think, is most bothered. He would rather go to a quieter lake. He wants to get away from people . . . so, perhaps, to understand them better!" Through his cheery mood came the note of sarcasm. "He will be President one day! So his wife teases him."

"Does she like Näsijärvi?"

"It is her land and villa that was bought by her father. He is a very active man."

"Your mother was telling me."

"Yes, he's a rogue. But I very much like him. Perhaps he will be of great use to Olavi."

"What's his daughter like? Have you read her poems?"

"She's different." One could just detect his feeling, of uncertain, covert fascination. "I don't know her poems. I think they are rather modern. About drugs, one of them. About sexual life."

"Oh, does that help a would-be politician?"

He laughed, enjoying the dig at his brother. "You'll see," he stood up, his preparations finished, "she is different. Perhaps she is essential for Olavi. He is a lucky man." He went off abruptly.

We fished till the sun blazed in the sky. The concealing mists floated away from us, and we stood (at least I did) revealed to our prey. Aarne had changed to a larger fly, had come to the river and altered his cast, but our total catch so far was paltry—well, a good meal apiece, but nothing for the market. The minnow jar was reasonably full. "Good work," he laughed, his mouth twisting, for at that instant as I whipped the line back, smartly, and so as to return it along a narrow curve to just above the water (where, I had observed, one followed through to achieve a cast like a feather alighting) it caught in a tree. "How did that happen?" "Like this, you could do it." With his left hand he looped some line from his own reel, then raised his rod in the easiest of motions, though the fly seemed not to go behind his head, but was dipping then curving up to the right, and over the water; then he freed the held line, and the flies had settled like thistledown. "Years of practice, Aarne." I scrambled up the tree. We rested awhile and had our lunch.

"What time are we going down to see them?"

"I don't know." He was puzzling over the trout. The air was full of every kind of insect, but it was early in the year for the fish to be glutted. He was eager to achieve a full creel. "I think I shall borrow some of your minnows. If they fail, there is always maggot!" As a sportsman, he obviously liked to win. He finished with lunch. He had a dogged look.

He showed me how to cast with minnow, swinging the line then shooting it out so that a further length was drawn from the rod. He would fish below the bend; I could try the water opposite. I must remember to work the bait convincingly. Trout were observant, suspicious creatures. We parted. I was a tyro but I could additionally feel that he had set me going to increase the challenge. I suppose he wanted the catch for Anna.

I was feeling terribly impatient to meet her.

And Olavi.

The lakeside over there called.

I angled lazily. It was not too adroit. A snarl on the reel, slack line, short casts; but gradually, as no expert was watching, an easier personal rhythm developed, and lo and behold, a trout bit. The bait was taken. I tightened, without realizing it, and the fish was straining up and down stream. Gently, firmly, I played the little fellow, wondering where my old scruples had gone; I released him, to fool him, I hauled him back. He was hooked, so why not end the fight quickly? But wasn't that also the tyrant's argument, the rapist's argument with country-lane girls? Was I frightened to return his liberty to him, now that things were this far? Through traces of buried primeval instinct?

As he surfaced, I pulled on him steadily and landed him, and hit him on the head with the stone I had ready. Best perhaps not to think about it.

On the distant lake the boats were buzzing. The forest between was a wad of silence, fringed with a thick curtain of insects. It was a hazy afternoon, a good time for sleep. How distant now were the winter snows! An occasional car came down the road, screaming as though for a forbidden frontier; then the silence returned. The lake sounds faded, were caught within the ripple of the river. One looked again, past the dance of mayflies, past weed and stone to the thin green depths, and of course down there the trout were lurking. They would have gobbled at anyone else's minnows. I was sorry now I had hit him on the head; I might as well have returned him to his mates. That primitive fear of other life! That inescapable half of the hunter.

Obviously bothered by no such qualms Aarne, when I joined him, had filled the creel. Small fellows mostly. He was just landing one, inserting his thumb into the mouth, then pressing the roof up against his forefinger till the spine gave with a tiny crack. I added my victim. No point thinking further. No point in imagining miniature Belsens. We gathered the gear and loaded the bike and, leaning into the cool pure air that washed the river heat away, slid through the intervening belt of woodland, and came bumping down a track to the lake.

"Many houses," said Aarne. Despite the bumps he was increasing speed, roughriding our approach. The trees continued thick to the water, but on all sides villas appeared that were swallowed up as soon as we had passed. Villa, the word invariably preferred by Finns to describe their summer hideout, equally meant a chalet or cabin, or small lodge, or simple hut, companioned, of course, by a second hut, the important one, the sauna. Most of these properties bordered the lake, if not actually along its front then around some unexpected inlet where the shore doubled back on itself. The main track fed them all, with cars parked in bays, rather than fell more trees to force a passage. We snorted through, propelled by eagerness, though the nearer we actually got to the lake, blazing deep blue against the wafery sky and shimmering with the day's unbroken sunshine, our noise was engulfed by that from the water. We couldn't yet hear the radios and record players with their currently screaming pop singers, though perhaps Aarne's ears were alerted for them, but off the water itself came a roaring, a ripsnorting and high-pitched sizzle as of monster hornets at bay. We had reached the shore. It was a modern playground.

True, Anna's villa, Olavi's villa, was a little further on in a private creek, with nothing beyond except the thinned-out forest and arable land of the local farmer, its green refreshing among pine and birch; and they had a southern prospect away from the area most favored by the speedboat fanatics. Still, it was hardly dreaming Finland. The noise came through. It pinned one to other people's exertions. "Oh yes," said Aarne, not minding it at all, seeming to absorb it with the same facility as fitted him into a silent landscape, "it is the weekend now. Many people here. I think, Anna is waiting for us. She has been swimming."

A thin woman, with slightly heavy legs, with a thickness also about her face that otherwise shone with warm intelligence, had just clambered out of the water, had noticed us and waved invitingly. That wave in itself dismissed inhibition. She had lit a cigarette. She called, her face shaded as she was caught by a hard burst of coughing, "Come on . . . on. I've been waiting for hours." She spoke husky English. Her voice was rough. Her eyes again faced us; clear, mirthful—reflecting, perhaps, the swim she had just had, for there were shadows behind if one looked closely. She was not yet thirty yet her youthful beauty had long been refashioned to a drier style. She waited with a restlessness that challenged. "Come on, Aarne. Have you brought me a present? Two presents, as you've brought me a guest."

Aarne, though she was no young popsy, was enraptured. This was Anna, the Karelian in the family.

Aarne swam with the excellence expected. Laboriously trying to follow his dive, the pressure drumming against my ears, I saw him glide, twisting and dipping, with the same ease as the fish we had been stalking; and out past the rocks, where the first shelf ended and the lake abruptly and dimly deepened, there was a flick of fins and watery eyes beamed across our path, and understanding that we were visitors, not predators, they flicked nearer, and aslant, and forward, probably amused when we had to surface.

Up in the air there was golden sunshine, and the gala commotion of outboard motors. Metal and paint and canvas shone. A miniature regatta was homing south. A white beetle came smacking toward us, a maniac bouncing to left then right across the wash of other propellers.

Enough. We swam back to the creek.

Anna had put on jeans with her bathing top. She had made coffee. We sat on the terrace. There were a few rocks, the reeds, and the water. When they had first come here, it must have been ideal, with Olavi's sauna just beyond the rise, facing east for the hour of sunset and the meditative expanse of lake. Only six years ago, Anna was saying, the land had been cheap, the farmer grateful to supplement his meager capital. Not now, though, good heavens not now; the price had risen five to ten times, the farmer was always reminding them of this and of how much, retrospectively, he had lost. He had bargained harshly in recent deals. People now said the top had been reached, that it was cheaper to invest in a car and go further. The young generation in fact was saying that it was cheaper, and nicer, to go to Spain.

No, she personally didn't mind the noise . . . it was only at weekends that it irritated . . . on some days the lake was silent. At crayfish time they had wonderful parties, visiting around. Olavi didn't like it. He was in the sauna (to Aarne's enquiry); did we wish to join him?

We were content with her.

Anna Suusanen. The more she talked the more she

suggested a second personality that was available once the mood was right, but that didn't enter into general conversation. Except to watch, note, consider. She basked a little in her brother-in-law's gaze. For him she had just the right affection. She was talking to him rapidly now in Finnish, asking about "Kirsti." They exploded with laughter. Then Aarne, in English, was volubly apologizing, blushing, "We don't laugh at the fact of illness. Please. It is misfortune. But my aunt—I can't explain this . . . I only hope you don't think we are laughing."

"But we are laughing." Anna was precise. Her smile lit into his discomfiture. "The mad are only fractionally madder. It is wonderful that Kirsti at last can preach and speak out her visions—and have doctors and professors listening to her—and have your father, with his pride, humbly attending. You must agree, it's rich."

"Rich?"

"That's English, rather old slang for it being comic. 'Oh come, let us make a joyful noise' . . . did he really join in singing that with her? 'Pekka, for forty years I have had intercourse, on your behalf, with God Almighty!' —well, she is lucky. Why say she is ill? The only misfortune would be if your father was shamed back to the arms of the Church. He should beware of his sister. She hasn't given up."

"I think that's crazy."

"Any crazier than religion?" She lit a cigarette; she didn't offer the packet. The warmth of her smile was broken through by her rough, firm, dissecting manner. Aarne looked shocked, pleased, attentive. He looked younger listening. He got from Anna more than his night-school textbooks gave him. Primarily he got—to tear things to pieces . . . but not to love people the less. He naturally loved people. Was it safe to tear?

He was unsure. He was not in that way so concerned. He found her completely fascinating, though.

They talked on, mostly in Finnish. There was a lull on the lake. The sun was fading into a soft yellow light, the trees stood taller, it was just as warm, and the midges and the mosquitoes and the horseflies whirred. I lit a cigarette and thought back to my recent stay with the Stromfors family, thirty lakes or so to the south, at the point where sea and inland water among those offshore islets became interchangeable. That, mentally, had been a different world, because of its seignorial traditions and the bridging quality of its sympathies between this country and the rest of Europe; and indispensable it was to the totality of Finland, to the way the future revolves round the past and does not head in a straight line, but nonetheless this present scene, summed up perhaps in the sound of Finnish, the incomprehensibility of it, against the quietened lake and the serried trees and the endlessly soft midsummer dusk (and Olavi, of course, remote in his sauna); this, indisputably, was native. This was the peculiar face of Finland.

"I think you must excuse us talking Finnish." He was aware of it. She was unconcerned, her concessions being of a different kind.

"I like listening. I like to imagine you Finns are still in your Caucasian birthplace. You happen to be here around the Baltic, but so stubborn and dreaming a peo-

ple can hardly have been touched much by migration. I
hear your speech as sounds from the past."

"Oh, it is. It is the most ancient music. One needs
Swedish to fix terms of reference for a joint Nordic tax
inspectorate, but to comfort one's soul or to sing to the
wind, we have to use our Caucasian tongue!" She liked
the idea. She offered a cigarette, not noticing that I
already had one. "We have charmed these northern lakes
with it. Especially in my province of Karelia. Poor Russians, with their pedagogic language, they do not have
so good a key!"

"Are you furious at the loss of your country?"

"Personally, I am not furious about anything." Her
voice rasped slightly beneath her broad, clear smile. She
had a strong nose, short black hair. Then, yielding a point
to sociability, "Aarne, I think I must offer you a drink."
She smiled more gaily. She knew he didn't touch it.

With some alacrity she produced a bottle, said "Good
luck!" and drank the first few glasses quickly. Instantly,
a more mellow Anna burgeoned.

Some minutes later, with audible happiness humming
up inside her, she began to look into our plans. Aarne
(he hadn't mentioned this before) wanted to join the
midsummer trek to hear the Rolling Stones on the beach
at Pori—an addition to the usual rockets and bonfires. I
didn't. For a second longer she withheld any helping
hand, then was suddenly mentioning the bed I could
sleep in (at least till the morning, for they might have
a visitor), and that Marjatta had written pages to Olavi
so that I mustn't feel myself a stranger. (We both knew

that I was the hell of a stranger, but I could feel all the Suusanens watching, thinking, well, he has come in so far, isn't he going to get round her?—the one, I learned later, that Pekka called the gypsy, the gypsy among their Suusanen stock. While she, with the help of the akvavit, was building up toward a party—"so stay," she repeated, "we can chat all evening"—and the last of her defensiveness smoothed away.) "Aarne," she said, "can't you stir Olavi? I believe he must have fallen asleep."

But Olavi appeared just then from the sauna. He was not aware so far of us, but was looking with disgust at the lake's animation that, fitfully, was beginning to revive. Anna whispered, "He has taken to sitting at the back, and staring at the trees like a Zen monk!" As we stared toward Olavi, she refilled her glass. "Don't attract his attention," she whispered, "let us watch him." Aarne indeed was watching him, and skeptically, no doubt wondering how a man could pause before plunging into the water, then thinking, Oh, well . . . Olavi. Anna was watching, then closing her eyes, then opening them with dark private dreams. I was watching and becoming mesmerized—for there was Pekka, younger, sterner, perhaps half a foot taller, on the point, one would have said, of rebuking the world. At this distance, in outline, the very image! And with a more active span of years ahead of him.

To achieve what had once been foretold of his father?

8

THE WHITE NIGHTS OF JUNE

8

THE WHITE NIGHTS OF JUNE

promptly applied), causing no one embarrassment

THE farmhouse stood half a mile away, along a delightful summer path. Olavi slowed his stride for Anna, who was always discovering something new—a flower, an insect, something precise that she studied intently then remarked upon, in Finnish or English as the words came to her; then she pocketed it, or something in its place, to take to Pentti, who was playing at the farm. She always stopped at the hayfield, in front of one of the old log barns (disused since the farmer had built a new cattle shed with a large loft for the fodder), and cried—"Halfway! Stop for a minute." Then, "I think there's a gnome lurking in this one," or "There is Runeberg's Finland for you!" or "Olavi, persuade him to sell it to us—for our next lake. We could move it by tractor. Oh, I suppose we couldn't. It has to stay here" . . . and she would run her hand over the wood or lean back against it.

Olavi as usual would be rapt in thought, smiling with his faraway expressions, his shoulders slightly hunched as he walked. Vaguely toward her he extended tolerance, gratitude, and some deeper sympathy. If the smile faded he looked awkwardly taciturn—and at first I had supposed he resented my presence, on the walk and also down by the lake in the villa, the cabin, where we lived rather intimately; but no, he had shown this was not the case. His taciturnity and awkwardness, which seemed to catch him unawares and was out of line with his public self—though not, perhaps, with much in his background—was deeply established; and he would turn toward her, thrashing in himself like some dumb brute, to be freed of this affliction by her subtle magic. Which she promptly applied, causing no one embarrassment. She was the keeper of her husband's nerves.

For he, so impressive at first glance, and so tremendously ambitious as one got to know him, was also riddled with little complications. He would have been lost without Anna's understanding.

The walk, and also by this time of day she had a few basic drinks inside her, was relatively free of their underlying tensions. For of course there was Anna's side to it too. She was always at her peak when needed by Olavi, but got depressed when he retreated again, back to that lofty, smooth personality, as though back to his club or some corridor of power where women as yet were not admitted. It was difficult to see why she took it so hard —for she had plenty to do, her verse, her translations, the house and the child, her caustic conversation; and Olavi in any case would soon be calling—but the fact was that she did take it hard. She was immediately depressed. She looked thrown out of gear. One just got a glimpse of passionate bewilderment; then down came her mask of uneven civility; then she had a few drinks and felt better.

It would have been difficult to say which of the two of them was more dependent on the other.

Anyway, during the walk it was easier, marking a sort of intermediate position—as after a swim or a meal, or the sauna—for she had had a drink and they were going for Pentti and Olavi was even shyly admiring her, returning his gaze from some abstract horizon to the succession of little pleasures she discovered. Their villa by the lake too closely confined them; the walk pulled them out of themselves.

After the hayfield there was a clover patch and a recent sowing of oats and barley—with wagtails, and swallows, and a multitude of finches skimming into the radiant air; and next to that on a south-facing slope, glacially smooth and with glacial boulders pushed back along its edges, a modest sowing of northern wheat. It was un-economic to invest in a tractor, with everywhere the impediment of undrained ditches, so ploughing was done by harnessing a horse, with the women following in a line sowing; and at other times weeding and hoeing, and in between they cared for the animals, shifted dung and milk churns, and were as rugged as the men. Most Finnish farms were far too small judged by market considerations, and without the capital for necessary improvements. This farmer happened to be better off, not because of his mere thirty tilled acres, nor because of his dozen dairy cows grazing for the brief summer months outside, but because of his forest, disproportionately large, and in par-ticular because of where some of it had stood, before he had sold out to developers.

As we reached the farm, first the old windmill, then the threshing shed, then a two-story outhouse where the lads and girls used to mate in spring and in fear of the farmer's stick if he caught them, then the new shed, then the house itself with its barricade of logs beside it, we usu-ally met Pentti unexpectedly. They adored Pentti, both loved to spoil him, but they equally encouraged his independence, which sent him scampering daily to the farm. "He is putting on weight . . . he looks taller, stronger . . ." was also a part of Anna's small talk.

"Look, here he comes"—and he was off as swiftly, after

the children or they after him, the old woman exclaiming as they whirled around her, and around the ladder at the side of the house leading up to the roof and chimney, and around the willows and off to the sauna; or they were splashing in the brook, where a split second before not a child had been in sight. Pigs and chickens trotted after them, then gave up before such swiftness. "Pentti," cried Anna, then laughed, helpless. Olavi soberly beamed his pride.

"Here is more of Runeberg's Finland," she remarked, for one little boy who came running more slowly had an unchanging, inbred grin on his face. "They used to be so cut off in winter. It's different now, with television." Above the farmhouse, the television mast.

The farmer looked cagily pleased to see us. On my first visit he had sat there in silence, oh, for five minutes, withholding a greeting, seemingly to test my vanity. I had not looked put out, so had been accepted. But this was as nothing to their experience of whole summers of prolonged chilliness. For even before Anna's father had appeared, the farmer had nursed a grudge against Karelians—because, having surrendered land, maybe peaty swamp but nonetheless land, to the refugee resettlements of the forties, he had seen the value of his State compensation dwindle in the inflation of the fifties— and then, to top this, her father came, a seemingly very forthright gentleman, saying straight out that the lakeshore was valuable and so worth the high sum he was offering, the sort of sum no man could refuse. But in retrospect . . . the offer had been nothing! The farmer still balefully looked through Anna.

Then, Olavi. Olavi was a townsman, a Social Democrat, and a college lecturer, the sort no doubt who would put on airs. The silent treatment had been lengthily applied —so lengthily that even Olavi, a Häme man, had begun to wonder if they had not strayed into a praying-sect household. It had only been after his return from lecturing for an exchange year in the United States (with an informative chat on American farming—to this farmer, like describing Mars), and Pentti had been growing, and the educated couple had convinced the farmer that they weren't looking down on him (though he, it was clear, looked down on them), and Olavi had added to the size of the villa by building another room himself (the farmer inspecting and helping with the roof) that friendly relations had been established. Eggs, milk, butter, and cheese, various parts of pig, salads and vegetables, had suddenly become twice as available. An occasional wild duck or hare had been dropped into their larder.

He received us in the kitchen living room, a large dog sprawling at his feet. On the table were slices of sausage, a bowl of butter, and black rye bread. He didn't invite us to sit and eat, but if talk started up then some eating followed. He had a strong old face with a white mustache, and a calm, level, suspicious stare. Still, inevitably, there were some moments of silence, to settle us down perhaps to his mood, and again to surmount the hump of the past; then he and Olavi exchanged observations. Nobody else uttered a word. His wife looked in, to serve if required—coffee, or thick cranberry tea— then sat in the shadows or returned outside to where her mother and daughter-in-law sat, admiring their latest woven rug. Anna on one occasion joined them and there was a softly courteous flow of talk. Anna adapted to every company, while always honestly giving her views (I think she did, I think this was intrinsic); while Olavi, rather rigid in manner, twisted his words as he best thought fit. Telling us afterwards what he had been saying (or, defending himself, in English, to Anna), the politician in him grinned at his deceptions.

The farmer tended to reiterate grudges and to pour scorn on city thinking. All but one of his children had deserted him, complaining of the farm's servitude only to become serfs in factories, clocked in to a fixed daily pattern. The independent Finnish yeoman had at last become the property of masters! It was the farmers who in the Winter War had saved Finland's freedom. Factory serfs didn't know about fighting. He evidently relished this word "serfs" to describe city people: for they had lost their country birthright. "Look you," he challenged Olavi, "you come to the country, all you people do, to keep your sanity. It's only madness reigning in the towns. And here you complain about the noise on the lake. You don't like machines, either."

"You are right." Olavi admitted he had said, "I don't like machines on holiday. I would rather live by the light of a candle, on a silent lake, fishing and resting."

"Oh, they've spoiled the fish here! The other morning I came on a pike in a net, thrashed itself to pieces. No thought of how to do it. They've dirtied the lake. And these are the people who think they have the right to vote for a change of government! Irresponsible. It is only the farmers who understand stability. We've given you the Paasikivi-Kekkonen line; it is we who have settled the question of the Neighbor. Are you Social Democrats thinking of stirring up that nest, endangering us again? You realize that you are a pawn of the Communists. I mean, our local fellows. You have to outbid them. Your entire life in the towns is cancerous."

"So how did you answer that one, Olavi?" Anna, glad to be receiving his account of it (the day she had sat outside with the women), yet intelligently scornful of his views too—"because," she had said apropos of politics, "it is usually a refashioning in trivial terms of the serious problems you run away from"—poured us each a drink, and relaxed in her chair. Pentti was in bed. Dinner was over. We were sitting on the terrace in the weirdly lit evening. The boats had mostly quietened by now.

Olavi smiled, averting his gaze. Calm within himself for the moment, he could play shy of her "possessive" manner. He edged away from the slightest indication in her tone or face of any wish "to claim" him. Anna shrank fractionally. If he was sensitive, so was she to these minute rebuffs. She took a deep swallow, and steadied her smile. "Come on, Olavi, couldn't you reply to him?"

He never hurried to speak. He let your curiosity gather. "Oh yes," he said, "I answered him. It became interesting. I showed him that he also renders to Caesar what is Caesar's due. These farms live by Co-operative arrangements, for credit, milk marketing, and so on, which is highly centralized, a city activity. He looks, I might say, to your father, a capitalist, for help to go into the broiler industry. But that by the way. It was enough really to remind him of how much townsmen have paid for his forest. Could he have sold this shore to country-men? As for politics . . . the Agrarians are so primitive . . . it is we, not they, who are the center Party, central, that is, to Finland's development. Although, I didn't mention my own position. . . ."

"What is that, Olavi?" I dared to question him, it having taken some days, civilities apart, to reach this point of familiarity. When I had tried once before, he had looked evasive, hurt, concerned with some speck on the horizon. Each evening he took me to his sauna, but to reduce me to his own state of reserve. His father, Pekka, except on those occasions when furiously determined not to speak, was incomparably more accessible.

"My own position"—after another pause, knife edge this time between words and total silence—"is that of the younger generation. We reject the old thinking of our chiefs." He looked towards Anna, with a tremor of confusion—"Yes," he hurried on, with a gathering rapidity, "we are not so frightened to work with the Communists. If, it is agreed, we must respect the Soviet Union . . . which today the Democrats officially accede to—the sign, at long last, of their political maturity . . . then equally we must respect the Communists here. . . ."

"No, Olavi, really, that is an illogical deduction. You should see that. *Pravda* may say so—but only so as to destroy Finland, I find you naive there, dear, really." She never, in English, called him more than "dear." No darlings, loves, sweethearts. They circled around each other demurely. They didn't exchange little open-air kisses.

He rolled on smoothly—"so after the election, which

we shall win, it is almost certain that some posts must
go to the Communists."

"God help our country!"

"Anna, you are childish." But he looked pleased. Argument pleased him. He fenced her off. He was inviol-
able here.

"You know, it is only because you have calculated
that this is your best ladder in the Party. Once at the
top, you will speak differently." For a moment she was
really sharp, exposing him.

But he blithely absorbed it. His round coconut head,
with the brown fringe of coconut hair, smiled all of a
piece. He was urbane, if secretive. "You will see that
you are wrong. A new generation is doing the thinking.
Why should we be bullied by our elders? Who every
year get more right-wing, and will end by tying us to
the bourgeois parties?" Then, just as he crowed un-
abashedly, the tremor returned and the onset of awkwardness. He looked puzzled, unsure of what he had
just said. Further words wouldn't form on his lips. It
was as if he had received an ancestral warning or felt
the sudden blight of guilt. He appealed to her.

"Olavi, you were telling us about the farmer, about
his prejudices. Isn't it really to do with his children? His
wife was saying——"

"Yes, yes. I understand. I understand, you know, about
him." He clicked, with difficulty, into this other continuation. Then he speeded up, grateful, "Yes, dear, I
know. He is making his will and he can already see they
are going to fight over the forest, what with the varying

site values. He doesn't want the farm broken up, so the oldest boy should pay the others out, with State help; but will they agree? There is no law yet to enforce it. He distrusts them. He says he would hand the farm over now, if it wasn't for the fear that they would kick him out. It would not be unusual. Farm life's so primitive. The sooner we industrialize the farming system . . ." He shook his head. He was speaking mechanically.

"I suppose, eventually, everyone will live in towns, even in Finland. . . ." One wanted to help him.

"In computer stations, in regional laboratories . . ." She also was trying, smiling mysteriously. Olavi was still sinking into silence. His disturbance was tightening not loosening its grip. He was beginning to look inwardly paralyzed.

His signals to her were weak, disconnected. He had lost color. He was grave, immobile.

She spoke to him in Finnish, and caught his attention. She left her drink standing in the glass, something she rarely could bear to do, and led him up the rise toward the sauna. They stood staring at the lake, then went indoors.

It was almost embarrassing to see her face. Her clear exultation in power. The compensating moment, the feminine reality, that bestowed a beauty and a fluency on her beyond even that of her warm intelligence. While he, always a dignified figure, followed in silence, ensnared, but already finding the way forward again.

It didn't get much darker that night. They had left the bottle so I quietly finished it. The lake turned to a smudgy white, as did the light between the trees, an atmosphere as much as a color. One of the long-prowed boats was out, without a motor, with two rods fishing. They might be after pike at this hour, with perch and other small ones as a bonus. A cry occasionally came over, and a far-off trickle of music. The unending twilight was hushed, vast, speaking again of this northern country.

I woke up chilled. The same light, and silence.

Olavi, as I've mentioned, was keen on the sauna. In Helsinki, rushing to lectures and committees, he could not get to it as often as he wished; he was driven, he admitted, to replenish his forces by remembering the peace and beatitude of the holidays, attained in his own smoky little hut—for of course for himself he had built a smoke sauna, and gladly paid the higher insurance; and inside its walls, though the buzz from the lake was clear enough to my ears, I don't believe he heard an outward thing. He was immersed in the ritual, in the mood it induced. Naked and sweating, his hairy body looking now like an elongated coconut, he was perfectly withdrawn, poised and strong. He seemingly never shared the sauna with Anna. She did have saunas, Pentti with her, but not with Olavi; he sweated alone. He beat himself with a mindless joy, with whisks collected from the young leafy birch, which he chose and bound sometimes late at night as though that hour imparted special qualities. He oozed and dripped; he slid into the lake. He returned to the porch and sat unhearing—well, with hearing unfocused, as though the motorboat roar was a function of some private space capsule from which he was surveying the kingdoms of the earth; for the difference was immediate when he did awake, and abruptly saw the scene in front of him. Then he was vexed. He viewed it pedantically.

Though he also stayed strong, renourished, he could glance down to where Anna was sitting, or shelling peas or teaching Pentti to swim (I am thinking of my seventh day there, when Pentti didn't go to the farm but was lost in a sudden craze for swimming), and look away again, detached and confident. The sauna was Olavi's stronghold. Anna really had nothing comparable.

This particular day she was in a black mood. Olavi had been strong for hours, and a bit preposterous discussing his ambitions. He never spelled these out exactly, but they emerged from his more confident comments. I kept on saying to each of this couple that I really must be returning to Tampere, but they both said no, stay a little longer. Anna wanted somebody there to whom she could be her unattached self, while Olavi, when strong, reveled in an audience, and when in that state blithely silenced Anna, silenced her own more tentative thoughts concerning life and human vanity or the more specifically literary problems she was exploring, and he crowed away, and conceivably he liked a spectator to see that he had this sort of power. He was not a particularly tactful person. Though his downfall came not the less unfailingly.

He was strong, she was furious—though she hid it from Pentti, whose body she jostled as they slid in the water;

then she took him to the kitchen for a man-size tea—
and it was certain to be a squally evening. Simplest really
if he caved in. But, as soon as the sauna trance had worn
off, Olavi, surveying his wife from the stronghold and
perhaps feeling it polite to put me wise, remarked, "Tomorrow my father is coming. He has sent a message. There
are new developments. He and my mother will spend the
day here. Anna is always nervous before that."

"But don't they stay with you each summer, for a week
or two?"

"Oh yes, we settle down. Anna is basically devoted to
them. It takes a day or so of adjustment."

"But are they intending to stay on now? You will need
my room. . . ."

"No, no, we have a tent. Marjatta will be coming,
you know, later. Toivo and Helmi sometimes stay over-
night. We sleep in the sauna. We don't mind the hard
ground. You must not conclude . . ." As he caught
Anna's voice, rasping and heated, coming from the kitchen,
he smiled as though to soothe away her anger; he was
so serene, so immaculately whole. He returned to a
remark he had been making earlier—"Yes, a third of
the electorate now are in their twenties. We must speak
for them. We who think the same. My father's generation
is remote."

"But it is his generation of Social Democrats—and I
agree with you, that you are going to win the 1966 election—who have done the spade work. It is their trials
and their evolution that will be attracting votes. Not
your ideas. Olavi, forgive me, but couldn't this return
you to the debacle of 1918? Even if ultimately you have to

work with the Communists, isn't it wiser to wait fifty years, and to consolidate your 'center' status? By then, they will be more like other people."

"Oh, will they change?"

"But you are claiming they have changed. Leave them to change a little bit more."

"But meanwhile it is undemocratic to exclude them."

It was extraordinary to observe his confidence. We left these words floating on the breeze. In other countries such words had been mooted. Anna said it was his experience of the States, where, as a Finn, he had been condemned to a barrage of anti-Soviet propaganda, that had opened him to the Communist line. (He had even worked off his American accent, and spoke English in the European way.) He was certainly, when strong, unresponsive to argument, the experience of the past or even moral factors—and this might propel him upward in politics if he took the plunge or, rather, the countdown, but then, he was not continuously strong. He was not his father. He would be much mistaken if he saw himself as outdistancing his father, of achieving what the old man had balked at. He was not what the first stern glimpse of him had suggested. Though when strong he was unrelievedly ambitious.

When weak, it was doubtful if he had any politics. When weak, he just wanted Anna.

That evening her temper did not fade away. Olavi remained quiet, Olympian. She read to Pentti, who then in his pyjamas continued to grub among the trees. She clattered some food onto the table. Anna was conceivedly a brilliant cook but by the lakeside she kept things simple; one day it would be ham and pickles, another it would be omelets, a third fish soup. Both she and Olavi knew how to fish, not with Aarne's elaborate preparations, but by hooking worms to a length of line and leaving this over a forked stick, till a jerk signaled some small capture. Olavi spoke of carp he had caught, after weeks of studying their psychology, but this was merely in his general conversation that on evenings like this flowed serenely.

She said, "What shall I give them tomorrow? Whatever it is, your mother will pity you. Milk, the mother symbol, of course . . . without which no Finn feels safe! Have you remarked how our modern societies are becoming inflated suckling machines? As if that will help with the real dangers!" She cast a scornful eye, as if Olavi's pretensions would not save him from the future she saw. Earlier in the day she had remarked to me, "It is not as if we shall be extinguished by flames, but by the necessities of our evolution. It is speeding up, we are getting closer to whatever follows after us. We shall be relatively like dogs then, shan't we, museum pieces, all our niceties in vain? Who will then care about the human God?" She had been getting very low that day.

She went on now, "But at least stop your mother from saying that I neglect Pentti. You also like to see him independent. I am quite willing to have a dozen children —if that topic comes up too. I have tidied away my notebooks, so nobody has to enquire what I am writing. What are they coming to see us about, anyway?"

"I think to arrange about their holiday."

"Oh yes, well, that is different. Once they are here, I find it restful. Your father, Olavi, is a wonderful man."

"Yes, we know. Mother told us that with our prayers."

There was a shade of a tremor, but somehow he resolved it. He continued to observe her with a subtle placidity.

She smiled. She saw that it would be a draw that evening. She said, "Shall we stroll up to the cemetery?"

Pentti was left to put himself to bed. If he did get scared he could scamper after us. Already he could track like an Indian brave, though his five small years had been mostly in the city. They didn't fear he might fall in the water or otherwise harm himself. He was a sensible chap. He grinned contentedly.

We walked up through the trees, away from the farm, along a path bordering other properties. Because of the lake still glinting behind us, with the late evening sun still sinking to the north, still fully illuminating Lapland, it was just possible not to get lost; for otherwise all around us was forest, inscrutably the same, with dips and turns that soon were leading wherever they chose. Once we did go in a circle, though that was partly through following a frog in and out of the sweet-smelling pines. "Silly of me," admitted Olavi, "Aarne can read the forest like a book. As children we used to blindfold and drag him in a *kelkka,* a chair toboggan, for miles, then let him go. He got home first. Pentti is like him. An ancestral quality. Marjatta and Helmi and I haven't got it."

"Nor me," murmured Anna. She was picking, in a dell, from a sudden profusion of lilies of the valley. "It's odd," she said, as we regained the path, "to think that a hundred years ago we Finns—I don't mean the Swedish Finns —were still the same trappers and peasants that we had been throughout our history. Actually I think we started as fishermen. We survived because we were never too united, and always knuckled under to others. Admit, we haven't changed too much. We are a study in the survival of lesser men. And the luck, of course, of having landed up here, in a not madly desirable country."

"Don't you love it, Anna?"

"Oh yes, I love it. I am part of it. I am trying to be objective."

"I don't care for the Swedish Finns." Olavi for once sounded mean. He had a heretic-burning expression. "We should be thankful that the Russians saved us, when they took us from Sweden in 1809. That was the springboard of our advancement. In the future, too, in my opinion, Russia will give us more than Scandinavia."

Anna was silent. We had found the cemetery, near the main road, close to the church. Here the farmer came each Sunday, and all his household, dressed in black. The church was an old, partly timbered construction with a separate wood belfry. The cemetery was small but perfectly kept. The graves, unless they had simple stones, simple crosses, marking the spot, were surmounted by a medley of devotional gardens with bushes and rock plants and flowers, and often the semblance of a miniature landscape molded out of earth and pebbles that might represent some local haunt to which the dead would be happy to return. Anna said that beneath their Lutheran black the farmers still listened to departed spirits. In Karelia the ancestral cult had been the very basis of the living family. As sweet a thing to believe, anyway, as what had tried to take its place.

"I have never understood, Olavi, why you haven't formally left the Church."

"Because that is still viewed so badly." He explained to me, "Before 1923 it was actually illegal—unless one was a Jew, or an Orthodox like Anna!—not to belong to the State Lutheran Church. Even now, ninety-five per cent of Finns, with the proportion hardly lower among Communists, are registered as Lutherans. One can resign today, but it is a public process. It doesn't help one's career to do it."

"Oh, your career! Though you have got a point there. Holiness opens every door in this country, while obscuring the minds of those who practice it." She was still out of sorts, ready to needle, but less persistently. She was dreaming now, her hands full of flowers, and walking just a little ahead of us. "I think," she said, "that I want to go back. If this holy Finn can find the way!"

Then she found it herself. Her thirst guided her.

When I went to bed they were sitting by the water, drinking and squabbling so very softly that it was no louder than the lap and suck against the shore.

I looked out later—at some hour after midnight, when the sun was already stirring with morning, imposing it on the nocturnal whiteness, so that out of the oily, unreflecting lake golden shafts of mist arose—and there she still was, drinking, but alone. Like a grumpy magician at the lakeside.

The stage was set but the cast was incomplete. Due about three, they were still absent at five. Olavi, who had handled the prologue superbly, seeing even to the cooking of the chicken that he and Pentti had brought from the farm, seeing to the suana, calling on a neighbor who had access to an illicit still—Olavi, displaying a practical vein that seemed to feed him with secret amusement, was becoming nervous. "It is because of midsummer—that upsets people's sense of time. Even my father's. He and Toivo together, they . . ." But he didn't continue. It had shown before now that he resented Toivo's easy relationship with his father, though when Anna had challenged, "You could go more to Tampere," not caring that she said this before a stranger, he had answered in a solemn, averted way, "It does not seem to get us anywhere." Though today, however tense inside over the coming encounter with his parent, he had been setting the stage with urbane good will.

It was only now, waiting, ready, that he was beginning to fidget and to look overstern.

Anna all this while had been asleep. Well, she had woken up once, seen that Pentti was happy, had excused herself with "Today I suffer," and had retired again. She had looked ghastly.

He was now determined to wake her properly. He called her in Finnish, cajoling, then crossly striding in and out of their room. He said in English, "One must face reality . . . that is what you are always telling me." Both of them were adopting the habit of speechifying to each other in English, enlisting the guest's attention for their arguments. They could do this without it causing embarrassment because, fundamentally, they were so attached.

She appeared, complaining, "It is one of those days

when I just don't feel allowed to come alive. It has nothing whatever to do with your family. I am in reverse. I drank too much."

"Well, please, have another small drink. But, get ready, quick. You can see they should be here. I have the sauna ready."

She smiled at his nervousness. "Oh, I'll be all right." She went into the kitchen and clattered the casserole. There was a subdued laugh. She reappeared in the doorway. "Thank you, Olavi, you are very sweet." Then she came past in her bathing costume and went for a long exploratory swim. She dressed in jeans and a dark red sweater. "The weather is changing. The water's icy. Well, so, where is everybody?"

He sat fidgeting, querying her jeans, silenced when she asked what Helmi would wear; then they stared at the neutral and indeed changing sky, the cumulus piled high from the west; then Olavi again inspected the sauna.

Pentti asked something in his sharp, reedy voice, the phrases short and produced with circumspection. It was Pentti, not Olavi, who took after Pekka.

There was the sound of a car approaching from the woods, whining into a lower gear, handling the track at purposeful speed. "That is Toivo," she said, "our barracuda of the road! Well, I hope he spares me his attentions."

I smiled inquisitively.

"Oh, I know the producer whom Helmi would like to work for in Tampere. Of course she can't just now with a baby coming, but she talks about it. Toivo's way of warning me off is more or less to threaten to rape me."

"He is a bit aggressive."

"I should say! Politically, you know, he wants us in NATO. Last summer he ditched Marjatta, because for once she got a man for herself."

"Good for her!"

"Oh, the man was a rotter. A midsummer folly. But don't imagine that as a family we are all butter and holiness. . . ." She was standing up, getting ready to present herself, a demure flush masking her countenance. Olavi was striding back from the sauna. "At last!" he cried. Her fingers strayed toward the bottle on the table but she controlled them.

Pekka got out first and noticed the bottle and that some of the glasses had been used, but whereas ordinarily he would have stared meaningfully, not disapprovingly necessarily but levelly at the scene as though to hope that the drinkers understood their action, and Mrs. Suusanen pulling herself out behind him would have stared with foreboding, both of them now and he especially beamed a glance of unshakable charity. *"Autossa oli kuuma. Järven rannalla näyttää viileältä!"* he proclaimed—roughly, It was hot in the car. It looks cool by the lake! He shook hands with the three of us. He picked up Pentti—who stared at him with such solemn intensity that the likeness got through. *"Tuo naperohan on minun näköiseni!"* This little fellow looks like me.

But not today. Pekka was animated, his whole appearance bigger and fleshier, for all that he was wearing a thick check shirt instead of his usual bulky jacket; his

eyes were clear and edging to jokes; his mouth had lost
its contracted line and was wide, ready to talk to people.
His hand grip was of friendly iron. He was standing more
or less on one spot, as he always did, as though the
weight of his life did not allow of too much movement,
but he was disporting this weight with a new-found confidence. Some major milestone had been passed.

He went on talking about the lake, approving the
view, behaving much like anyone, I suppose, who after
a particularly trying year sees a well-earned holiday beginning; he lifted little Pentti up so the child could
get a better look at the boats, but there was more to it
than this—for he was back on form, a form, I could suddenly appreciate, that was closer to the irreducible Pekka
than anything I had seen during my stay. He had more
effortless energy. Simply that. He was off the treadmill
of sustained anxiety.

He was not hastening with an explanation. He en-
quired if the sauna were ready. He stared at Olavi, with
a kind of genuine wish to understand this slightly pallid
first-born, who was looking so terribly serious just now,
and who was so neatly dressed, so unnecessarily by the
lake. Anna he had swept with a stubborn, but also teas-
ing, interested glance. There was nothing apparently to
disturb his sense of ease. He looked up at the extended
roof appreciatively, giving credit where credit was due;
then, *"Mennäänkö saunaan?"* Shall we go to the sauna?
I walked beside him, and tried a little Finnish, at which,
swiftly, he essayed in English—"Your friend, you . . .
remember, Mr. Koivaara? Yes? It is right? He sends good
greetings. Okay there. Better. Mmm, difficult. Good."

He laughed with the impossibility of English. He gripped
my shoulder. "Now we go . . . into sauna!" A happy
bull, he strode in first.

Saunas greatly vary. Well, some smokers say that
every pipe and cigar tastes different. Every prayer meeting is different. A picture you love, or a poem, or a
woman, can be utterly different on successive occasions.
Your favorite food is never twice the same. Your habitual
walk. The moment of waking. Perhaps nothing twice
running can be a facsimile. Saunas certainly, in changed
mood and company, become almost contradictory experiences, for all the same sweating and beating and
washing.

Well, here was the lake and the little smoke sauna in
which, with Olavi, I had been pursuing Zen—not Lars's
Zen, the discarding of one's life-form to wallow thereafter
in the inner flux, but a more workaday notion of recharg-
ing one's forces (insights, ambitions, dependent on one's
style) by momentarily defocusing consciousness; but
today, with this inrush of extrovert vigor, Toivo as to
be expected neatly folding his clothes then marching
with bucket, soap and whisk as though drilled by an in-
structor's whistle, we became an outward-facing group,
limbering up as we harkened to the excitement of the
holiday world outside. We sluiced ourselves to feel fit
and clean. We plunged toward the other swimmers in
the water. We sat on the porch and remarked on the
steamer, that was raising a wave that delighted the speed
fiends; then, more slowly following, we watched the bun-
dle raft—of several thousand tree-length logs—being tugged
south to the Pispala tunnel.

Toivo, in Finnish, produced some numbers to do with timber expectations that year.

Olavi translated, with polite melancholy. He wasn't happy in this sort of sauna. Since his father's arrival he had been fading into silence, from the first burst of welcoming chairmanship through surprise to a kind of glazed unimpressiveness, as though that best fitted their view of him. He was paralyzed by some quality in Pekka. Toivo he ignored as far as he could. He was now giving to the numbers a curl of derision, as though to recall our contrasting memories, on other days, of the rafts floating by and the poetic simile he had employed then, talking of their further journey down the river, likening them to driven beasts, herded in the booms and bucking down the shoots, to be finally corralled at the coast, at Pori. He was not usually poetic in speech, so one guessed the words had come from Anna, but it was in the sauna that he was able to voice them. But not now, not in today's sort of sauna.

Sauna over—*"Sauna on vapaa!"*, so that the women could take their turn after us—we sat on the terrace and began drinking. Beer was tossed down, only Toivo limiting himself to raspberry syrup. "I am the driver," he explained, "and the punishment for taking one drink while driving is heavy. I would rather drive on roads than build them." "That is right," said Pekka, and quenched his thirst. He now had his eye more squarely on Olavi and something of his first animation had gone. Father and son looked bogged in their inability to find an easy way with each other. Anna said they always got over this, Olavi retreating to some youthful role. She,

for all her fears raised yesterday, was now acting in the
gayest of fashions, charming Mrs. Suusanen, delighting
Helmi. Helmi, like Aarne, was enraptured by Anna.

The women weren't long in the sauna. They rejoined
us on the terrace. Anna took a dark, deep look at everyone and departed to the kitchen, and one's attuned ear
knew the particular bottle she was opening. Mrs. Suusanen, who had brought more provisions, of fresh salmon and vegetables and cake and fruit, turned to play
with Pentti, all her bustle subsiding into simple grand-
motherly pleasures. Helmi observed this avidly, then
went off to Anna, pushing past Toivo. She was wearing
a bright Marimekko dress.

"And why is Aarne so late?" asked Pekka. "Nothing
begins till Aarne is here." His look continued to invigi-
late Olavi. His animated presence was coming back, as
the beer was replaced by akvavit, and he seemed on the
edge of making a statement. A more difficult exchange
in Finnish followed. Toivo decided to check the tire
pressures and look beneath the bonnet of the Saab, so I
joined him, though it was not very interesting, though I
realized that from here one could monitor the kitchen,
and at that moment hear Helmi, now employing Swedish as though it befitted such upper-class jinks, describe some youngsters' strip-tease party interrupted by
the parents returning home. One of the leading families
of the city. Known for always being on their knees to
God. To find their children, drunk, in an orgy, along
with girls picked up in a coffee bar!

"I could do with an orgy," Anna was commenting.
Toivo crispened with a look of fury.

Aarne arrived, with the usual tackle, and a creel of
fish, and much cheerful apology. He skidded up beside
the Saab, and sent a last blast of exhaust into us. "Sorry.
What a day! Toivo . . . hello!" His innocence restored
common sense. "Hello, Dad." This was still in English.
"Have you told the news?" He grinned infectiously.

"To Olavi, I am speaking." Pekka now looked flushed,
Finn-thick with successive quenches, but sturdy-eyed and
possessed by conviction; he was definitely in the middle
of a statement. "You tell, to English friend. No, I
through Olavi." But then he waved us away for the time
being.

So in that time Aarne, haltingly, enthused at the new
turn in their fortunes. The offer of land had been renewed—by the managing director himself at Stromfors
—and had been coupled with a very low interest loan
that would enable a good modern house to be built.
Aarne dwelt on the possibility of modernity as the fea-
ture that most interested him, the low lines and concealed
lighting, the mechanization and grouped controls. Also
he was thinking of Pyhäjärvi and the fishing to be done
direct from the house. But he conveyed that for his
father it had been a breakthrough—not just the actual
step of acceptance (with admission of accumulated eagerness at this point), but a blinding realization while doing
so that he, the old fighter Pekka Suusanen, was in fact
a manager from his head to his toes, that factories, like
armies, couldn't run without orders, and that if he hadn't
always been so obstinate he would have realized this
twenty years ago. He had seemed to shed his old skin in
a trice. Hence this new spurt of energy.

"So next he will become a director!" One could make this sort of joke with Aarne.

"Why not? I think other views are old-fashioned." Aarne liked this taste of success. He also set his sights high, though without the intermediate travail.

"Your mother is pleased?"

"Yes. She will stop working. The time has come. We are all pleased."

I looked toward Pekka. He was almost punching Olavi with the firm exultant force of his statement. He was raising his hand as though it held the scroll of God, the contents of which he would forever follow. Morality was not less stamped on his face. Morality had been more searchingly understood. Only vanity, perhaps, had blinded him till now, the vanity of a too fixed role in life. He was a broadened-out man. His strength had been returned to him.

Olavi by contrast looked silently flattened, as though his own role had been seized; but, noticing our eyes, Aarne's and mine, upon him, he said, in determined, explanatory English, "My father at last is receiving his due. It is part of our new Democratic position. He has been telling me, especially the Communists in the factory have congratulated him. He is sure of their support. A sit-down strike even has been averted, because they prefer his negotiating power. Also the directors, strategically, will listen to him. This foretells, as I have been saying, the course of a national Democratic government. I take this as a very good omen."

And Olavi, without looking further in our direction, took a deep swallow of akvavit.

The meal was ready. It covered the table. A side table was brought into use. Milk and syrups and wine and spirits mingled on equal footing for once. We started off with poached salmon, with plenty of summer dill, and lemon; then came Olavi's chicken—Anna, not seeing that Olavi was depressed, announced it as his, and added to his confusion, as Toivo taunted, "Does he do the cooking?" Anna froze him. She was well away, and so was Olavi, so were we all, except for Toivo, who had switched on a portable radio for company. Pekka was setting the pace with his drinking. As certain as it was a midsummer evening, Pekka Suusanen was going to get drunk. He was celebrating a moment of awakening—perhaps of saying goodbye to the past and to prayers offered beyond the grave, so naturally, it was his right; he was going out blind. His wife knew it and was charitably accepting it. Better perhaps where neighbors couldn't see him. Get it over, this monumental drunk, this drowning of every agonized passion that over the years had compulsively forged him; let him be free . . . to relax in old age.

Once again he surprised us. He had the powers of a bull. He absorbed the spirits, and flooded them with wine, and then, stuffing himself with chicken, and beans and potatoes and turnip and beetroot—all at that peculiarly Finnish speed that is unable to pause till the plate is empty, the food seemingly vacuumed away—he took a deep breath, sank the lot, and stood up to make a speech.

He spoke in Finnish, but he motioned Anna to translate for my benefit, and waited with beautifully ponderous satisfaction as she neatly and with scattered com-

ment did this, and he said—in the main, and as she chose
it, he said, "I ask God to look down on our gathering,
for it pleases Him that we are a family and here. I speak
for this family in asking His blessing. I give thanks for
this meal, and for this summer evening. It is right to
be in harmony with Nature. Summer is short in our
country, like our lives. We say Amen to His goodness to
us. . . ."

"So that ends God," she added, continuing, "I speak
first of my wife, for she has been by my side—a good
mother to you, and to Anna and to Toivo. Only Marjatta,
we remember, is absent. Your mother has worked long
for us all, and now is the moment when she claims rest.
I shall continue working" (a pause) "while I have
strength. Men must work . . . at their proper work" (a
square look at Olavi) . . . "but women have their home
duties. We think of little Pentti . . . and now Helmi
soon. . . ." Sighs and grunts of approval were rising
toward the speaker. He was flushed, redder than the salmon, but toughly continuing. His words seemed to battle
up from his belly.

"Now it's your turn," came the whisper; then, translating . . . "We have an English friend sitting with us,
whom I met long ago. I think it was twenty-five years
ago. In the middle of a war which . . . in modesty
we claim . . . preserved the freedom we enjoy at this
minute. Where is Anna's Viipuri now? Would this lake
not also have become Russian? We defended this future
you are now enjoying. If it be threatened again, we shall
defend again. . . ."

"Yes, yes, Toivo is saying and adding that he would

love it . . . and you seem to have got lost at that point, for we have progressed"; translating, "And I have fought against the bosses, for justice. Justice and comradeship are sacred to me. Have I fought too hard? No. I say no. I have remembered your grandfather. It is right that we have fought and won this battle. Now we can each accept a place that fits our experience and our ability. Yet . . . each of us must remain vigilant!"

"Vigilant, vigilant!"—he is thumping that out. Well, he deserves a new deal; I am delighted. But my guess is, he'll be worrying again over something else within a month. Pekka—well, no Finn was born to exist easily. There is Kirsti to trouble him; he has not mentioned her. Perhaps that skeleton's gone back in the cupboard. For he is concluding translating, "I invite you next year, and you, our English friend, to a dinner like this . . . to be held, God willing, at the house I shall build . . . as I say, God willing, on Pyhäjärvi."

"So that's sewn up," she whispered, and suddenly, incongruously, her face flooded with tears.

"What is it?" they were asking, "Anna?" They turned to her, their kindness and solidity flushed from the dinner, trying to fathom their unpredictable Karelian.

"Well, I'm happy, of course. But I just remembered my own old home . . . well, I hardly even knew it!" She explained this in Finnish, reassured them, laughed. She was suddenly as harshly and incongruously laughing. "I'm the cuckoo, all right," she whispered, half-referring to the one we were hearing every day, and that she had already claimed was her soul calling her. "I'm the cuckoo in the family." She topped up her glass, taking quick advantage of their sympathy. She swayed to her feet. "I'll make the coffee."

But Mother Suusanen made it.

Toivo, to settle his nerves, took the car for an hour's spin on the roads. He and Olavi were poised to quarrel. Olavi was coming up fast, pugnaciously. He could not get any of them to discuss politics. He also looked primed to make a speech. But Anna and Helmi had linked arms and were giggling on a rock, Aarne near to them. I had followed Pekka. Olavi was left with the wreckage of the meal. His mother came and stood beside him, and after some thought stroked his shoulder.

Behind, that scene; ahead, the quiet lake, ruffled and blowing with damp warm air. A swan was nearing her nesting islet, her wings stretched up as she landed. It was darker this evening, with a thick pink light, purple where the clouds were gathering. The boats had all returned to their moorings; there were laughter and music but also pockets of silence from where one now knew houses to be. There was an air of restraint, of realization that inevitably winter must come again to round off this too short summer. In the uncertain light the colors of autumn, the yellows and russets, already trembled; and in the mind's eye, the diamonds of winter. The woods around were still curdled with heat, but new seasons prepared across the water. The sky was wider toward the west, and first from there rain was coming.

"It will rain," said Pekka. "That is right? It will rain?"

"Yes. That's right. You have a short summer."

"Yes." He brooded. He tried again in English, "Winter makes strong! Winter . . . Finnish people . . . they go together." He rubbed his two forefingers edge to edge. "You see in the war. The Winter War!" He laughed with pleasure, so much this evening pleasantly and worthily turning in his mind. "We are a winter people. It is good like that."

He stood happily facing the water, modest, decorous, his fires unflagging. I could feel his friendship unreserved toward me, but, true northerner, he made no show of it. He was staring to where a speck of a fisherman was setting up a net for the night, and his features took on scorn at the sight of it; then gloom, as he stared up at the clouds; then tenacity, as he adjusted within. Very quickly his usual Häme face, his enduring face, had taken over. One had to know what was still within him, singing and marching, to understand that face, not to find it too bleakly northern.

"Olipa hauskaa . . . että tulin tänne." The words, unexpected, in his language and out of that moment, had leaped to my tongue . . . I am glad that I have come here.

He replied as warmly. We shook hands. Then, swiftly retreating as though nothing had been demonstrated, we continued silently to view the lake. An uninflected silence, tranquil, serious, into which perhaps seeped a little Finnish melancholy, and an awareness of other worlds beyond us that touched us only to point the more surely to the duties and challenge of this one.

"The coffee is ready!"

We returned to the terrace, to the arena of family life.